EPIC ATHLETES
STEPHEN CURRY

Dan Wetzel

Illustrations by Zeke Peña

SQUARE FISH

Henry Holt and Company
New York

SQUARE
FISH

An imprint of Macmillan Publishing Group, LLC
120 Broadway, New York, NY 10271
mackids.com

Library of Congress Cataloging-in-Publication Data
Names: Wetzel, Dan, author.
Title: Stephen Curry / Dan Wetzel ; [illustrations by Zeke Peña].
Description: New York : Henry Holt and Company, [2019] | Series: Epic athletes
Identifiers: LCCN 2018039227 | ISBN 978-1-250-25062-9 (paperback)
| ISBN 978-1-250-29584-2 (E-book)
Subjects: LCSH: Curry, Stephen, 1988—Juvenile literature. | Basketball players—
United States—Biography—Juvenile literature. | African American
basketball players—United States—Biography—Juvenile literature.
Classification: LCC GV884.C88 W48 2019 | DDC 796.323092 [B]—dc23
LC record available at https://lccn.loc.gov/2018039227

Originally published in the United States by Henry Holt and Company
First Square Fish edition, 2020
Book designed by Elynn Cohen
Square Fish logo designed by Filomena Tuosto

3 5 7 9 10 8 6 4

AR: 6.7 / LEXILE: 1000L

For Allie

Also by Dan Wetzel

Epic Athletes
ALEX MORGAN

Epic Athletes
TOM BRADY

Epic Athletes
SERENA WILLIAMS

Epic Athletes
LEBRON JAMES

Epic Athletes
LIONEL MESSI

Epic Athletes
SIMONE BILES

118 05.3 118

1
Underdog

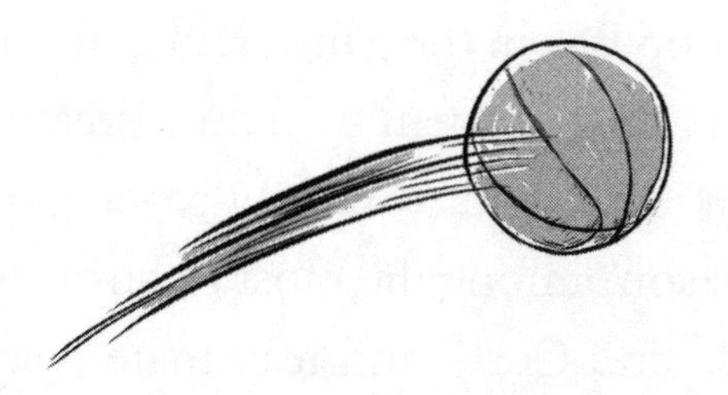

TWENTY THOUSAND CLEVELAND CAVALIERS fans stood inside Quicken Loans Arena and tried to distract Stephen Curry. They stomped their feet. They waved their arms. They cupped their hands up to their faces and screamed.

It was Game 6 of the 2015 NBA Finals, and Cleveland's J. R. Smith had just drained a three-pointer. A Golden State lead that only minutes before had stretched to thirteen points was now just four, 101–97. There were 29.0 seconds remaining, still enough time for the Cavaliers to mount a comeback. Golden State led the series 3–2 and was trying to win the franchise's first NBA title in forty years. The Warriors wanted to end the series right then, in this game, and avoid having to play a decisive Game 7. They didn't want to give Cleveland superstar LeBron James another chance to win it all.

Cleveland had all the momentum. It was up to Curry to stop it, win the game, and grab the championship that he had spent a lifetime dreaming about.

Golden State had won sixty-seven games in the regular season, among the most by any team in NBA history. Behind Curry and teammate Klay Thompson, dubbed the "Splash Brothers" for the way so many of their long three-pointers splashed through the net, the team had cruised to The Finals with a 12–3 record. It was expected to beat Cleveland handily, especially after one of the Cavs' stars, Kyrie Irving, was lost to injury.

Instead, LeBron raised his level of play and Cleveland took two of the first three games. To make matters worse, Steph, the best player in the league that season, was in a slump. His usually reliable shot was off. At the end of the Game 2 loss, he shot just two of fifteen from three-point range. He even tossed up an air ball, missing the rim altogether. "Shots I normally make . . . I knew as soon as they left my hand that they were off," Steph explained. "That doesn't usually happen."

In the media, there was talk that Steph wasn't tough enough for the big games and the pressure of the NBA Finals was getting to him. He had shaken that off and returned to form in Games 4, 5, and now Game 6. The Warriors clawed back and took the lead in the series. They couldn't imagine it all coming undone in the last minute.

Everything rested on the slim shoulders of Steph Curry, who had been fouled and awarded two free throws. If he missed one or both of the shots from the line, Cleveland still had a chance. If he hit them, Golden State was almost assuredly going to win.

With the pressure mounting and the noise of all those Cavaliers fans raining down on him, Steph walked to the free-throw line. For years he had dreamed of and practiced for this moment. His entire life he'd been told over and over the same thing by coaches, scouts, and the media—that he would never be good enough to be a great college star or NBA player, let alone the MVP of the entire league.

Too small, they said. Too short, they claimed. Too little, they argued.

Curry now stood six foot three and weighed 190 pounds. That was small by NBA standards. LeBron, for instance, checked in at six-eight and 265 pounds of muscle. Curry had always been undersized, though, and he adapted his game around that fact. He was sometimes the smallest kid on the court in middle school. As a high school sophomore, he said he was "a little scrawny kid, like maybe five foot six, five foot seven and 120 pounds." So he learned to shoot the ball with a high arc to avoid the outstretched arms of taller kids who would try to block his shot. By using quick dribbles and his speed, he found ways to create space on the court to get the ball up in the air and away from bigger players attempting to steal it from him.

He also knew that if there was one place on a basketball court where his height and weight didn't matter, it was the free-throw line. No one is allowed to guard you there. No one can stop you from hitting every shot you take. The free-throw line doesn't care who you are. It's just you, the ball, and the rim, fifteen feet away, ten feet in the air. In a sport with so much movement, it is the one time everything is the same, from grade school basketball to here in the NBA Finals. It's the one time the game stands still—but the pressure is still impossible to ignore.

Steph couldn't count the hours he'd spent perfecting his routine and shot from the line. He was never going to be a great dunker. He was never going to be able to muscle over opponents and score easily. He understood his strengths and didn't complain about his weaknesses. He knew he had to take points where he could get them. Besides, if bigger players were going to test his toughness and foul him, if they were going to attempt to bully him, the best revenge was to make both free throws. Eventually they'd stop or lose the game.

It started back in the driveway of his family's home in Charlotte, North Carolina. It continued through his days at Charlotte Christian School and then Davidson College, the small school that believed in his potential. It remained a daily habit across his first six years in the NBA, when many wondered if he'd ever become a star.

No matter how good Curry got, he never stopped working on the basics, and that meant free throws. The key to hitting free throws is using the exact same approach and technique on every shot, even before you release the ball. It was a lesson his father, Dell, taught him at an early age. If you are dedicated to your training, then you always have something to lean back on.

Dell would know. He spent sixteen seasons in the NBA. He was a great player, which was another criticism Steph heard growing up: He wasn't as good as his dad. Comparing a kid to an NBA player was unfair. How could a seventh grader, a high schooler, even a college player be as good as an NBA player? If Dell Curry weren't his father, no one would have compared Steph to an NBA star. He'd just be Steph. Yet that's what so many did. Steph heard it his entire life but never felt resentment toward his father. He loved him and loved the support he provided. These free throws were for Dell, too. Through all his years in the NBA, Dell was never on a championship team. This would be a title for the entire Curry family.

Steph knew that in these tense moments he needed concentration, repetition, balance, and follow-through. He was the best free-throw shooter in the league, hitting 91.4 percent of his attempts during the season. So even here, on the verge of attempting the most tense and dramatic free throws of his life, nothing changed. He went with what he knew best.

He stepped to the line and stared directly at the rim. He ignored the screaming fans, the waving arms, and the nervous teammates on the bench, who were silently praying that he'd make it. He took a deep breath and then exhaled to calm his nerves. He chomped on his mouth guard, which was hanging halfway out of his mouth, a habit he'd picked up through the years that now felt natural. "It calms me down," he explained. He took one dribble and then smoothly shot.

Swish.

The Cleveland fans groaned before again ratcheting up the noise and commotion. Maybe, they thought, they could rattle him and make him miss the second shot.

Curry reacted like no one was in the arena. He was just a kid all alone back in his driveway rather than one shot away from icing the NBA championship. He casually slapped hands with a few of his teammates and then stepped back into the routine.

Deep breath, exhale, chomp the mouth guard, one bounce, perfect form.

Swish!

Moments later the game and championship were won, Golden State 105–97. Steph congratulated James on a series well played, dribbled out the clock, and pointed up to the sky. He then jumped up and down and hugged his teammates.

"I'm just so happy, man," Curry said. "God is great."

The Golden State Warriors were champions at last, and Stephen Curry, the too-small, too-weak guard who no major college thought was talented enough to play for them finished with twenty-five points, eight assists, and six rebounds, including those clutch free throws in the clinching game. Amid the celebration he quickly found his father on the court and thanked the man who'd taught him that through hard work and deep belief he was capable of proving everyone wrong.

"It's an unbelievable feeling in that moment," Steph said. "I followed in his footsteps. I've talked about how impactful he's been in my life. Just being an example on and off the court of what a true professional is and how he raised me and my brother and my sister. So to be able to have that moment was special." He continued, "I can't be more proud of him as a father and a role model and example for me. I hope it made him proud tonight."

Later, Dell Curry would just smile about what his son had accomplished. It had been a long journey with plenty of hurdles to clear. All those years when he'd look at his son and hope he would hit a growth spurt. The rejection from the bigger college programs, the doubts from the media, and all the injuries and losses during Steph's first years on Golden State. When Steph was a rookie, the team had gone just 26–56, nearly last place in their division. It was typical for Golden State, which was never a power like the Los Angeles Lakers, Boston Celtics, or San Antonio Spurs. No one ever thought the Warriors would amount to much of anything.

How far he'd come.

Through it all, the plan the Currys believed in came together. Hard work gave Steph the sweetest, smoothest jump shot in the league. Steph, for years, took about 2,000 practice shots a week and at least 250 a day. He took so many his hands grew calloused like he was a construction worker. Endless hours of routine made him the NBA's best ball handler. He'd embrace dull drills of dribbling forward, backward, between his legs, sometimes with a ball in each hand, over and over. He was so good, fans began arriving well before the games just to watch him practicing and film it on their phones.

Meanwhile, all those who didn't believe in him gave Steph the fire to prove them wrong, to quiet them like he did all those Cleveland fans screaming for him to miss the free throws. Every day he got a little better. So did Golden State. What could anyone say now? Steph and his team were champions, the best of the best.

"Make me proud?" Dell Curry said when told what his son had said about him. "I hope I made *him* proud."

2

Growing Up

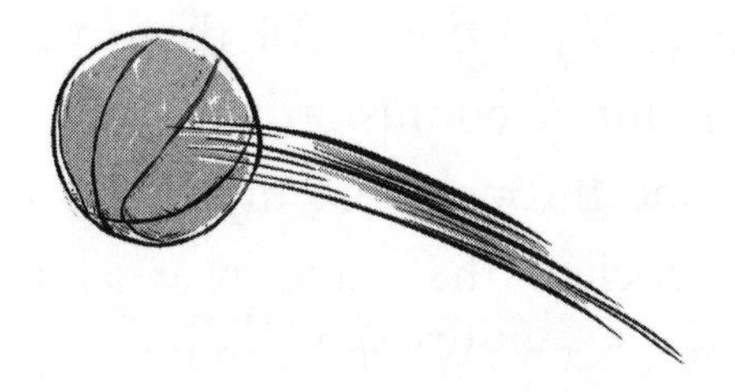

WARDELL STEPHEN CURRY II was born on March 14, 1988, a Monday, in Akron, Ohio. He was named after his father, Wardell Stephen Curry I, who was known as "Dell." Dell Curry was named after his father, Wardell "Jack" Curry, so he was just passing along the family name. The Currys didn't want to live a life of confusion where both were known by the same name, so their first son was immediately called by his middle name, Stephen. But not everyone followed that rule. Growing up, Steph's friends called him Wardell, often as a way of playfully teasing him because the name was old-fashioned.

The most confusing part, however, was the unusual pronunciation of "Stephen." Stephen is usually pronounced like "STEE-ven," like its other spelling, Steven. In this case, the name was pronounced "STEFF-in." All these years later, it remains a point of confusion.

"I've gone through that my whole life," Steph said. "It's spelled the same way as the normal 'Stephen' you hear." When he met new people who mispronounced "Stephen," he told them, "you can call me Steph [pronounced *Steff*]. That just works for both of us."

Dell was in his second season in the NBA when Steph was born. Drafted by the Utah Jazz, he was traded to Cleveland for the 1987–88 season. He and his wife, Sonya, lived in the Akron area, not far from the Cavaliers' arena at the time. They were newly married and young parents, Dell just twenty-three, Sonya just twenty-one. They were overjoyed at their baby boy, who would soon be followed by a brother, Seth, in 1990 and a sister, Sydel, in 1994. Coincidentally, less than four years earlier another future basketball player, one named LeBron James, had been born at the same Akron hospital ("pretty crazy," Steph would say later).

Unlike LeBron, Steph didn't stay and grow up in Akron. After just one year in Cleveland, Dell was picked up by the Charlotte Hornets, an expansion franchise that was about to play its very first season in a new arena in North Carolina. There was incredible excitement for the team, the first major professional sports franchise to find a home in the Carolinas. The Hornets led the NBA in attendance right away, even though it wasn't a great team at first. Within a few years, the Hornets reached the playoffs and the players became very famous in Charlotte. Dell developed into one of the best three-point shooters in the league, averaging double digits in points in nine of his ten seasons with the Hornets. During the 1993–94 season, he was named the NBA's Sixth Man of the Year, an award given annually to the best player in the league who isn't a regular starter. He retired as the franchise career leader in games played, points scored, and two- and three-point field goals made, though he would eventually be surpassed years later. He now serves as a television broadcaster for the Hornets, sometimes calling games featuring his own sons, Steph and Seth, while trying to not sound biased in their favor.

The life of an NBA family is exciting. The players are well paid. Everyone around town knows who they are. For the kids, there are games to attend and famous athletes to meet both on their father's team and the opposing one.

There are also drawbacks. The job requires a great deal of effort, not just long road trips away from the family but endless hours of practice, individual work, and training. Dell Curry was a loving and caring father, but he wasn't always able to be with the family. The night Steph was born, for instance, Dell played a game in New York. He scored fifteen points, but the Cavs lost to the Knicks. Cleveland had a game the next night in Chicago. Rather than travel with the team to Chicago, Dell caught an early flight to Cleveland and drove to the hospital in Akron to visit Sonya and see his firstborn son. He then quickly left to fly to Chicago and met his teammates for another game.

That was the NBA life, though: constant travel, practice, and games that couldn't be missed. The job of parenting often fell to Sonya, who had to make sure homework was done, discipline was laid down, and manners were minded. Sonya grew up in Radford, Virginia, a small city in the southwest part of the state. She was also a great athlete when she was young, eventually playing volleyball at Virginia Tech. In her family, hard work was expected. So was a commitment to faith. While her kids were born into privilege as the children of an NBA star, Sonya was determined to have them learn the same lessons that she had learned. She was strict. She was not going to raise spoiled children. Household chores were mandatory, and once, in middle school, when Steph didn't finish doing the dishes, his mother made him sit out a basketball game to learn his lesson. "I went to school and had to tell my team, 'Hey, guys, I can't play tonight,'" Steph recalled. "Four dirty dish plates in the sink, and I didn't get it done. You learn priorities and understand basketball is a privilege. It can be taken away."

For Steph and Seth, the biggest thrill was getting to go to Charlotte home games. They usually had great seats, met famous players on both the Hornets and other teams, and often shot baskets on the court before the game or at practices. They hung around the locker room and became friends with the players.

The problem was that the games started late and Sonya Curry wouldn't let them go on weeknights because they needed to be up early the next morning. "She'd always say, 'school night,'" Steph said. So they would wait all week for a Friday- or Saturday-night game and go see their dad in action.

While Dell was a professional basketball player, he didn't push his children into the sport. The family had a hoop in the driveway, but the kids gravitated to different passions. Steph played Little League baseball, youth football, and lots of golf. Steph had a very smooth golf swing at an early age. He played golf in high school and developed into a great golfer as an adult. Many in the golf community believe that if Steph had decided to concentrate on golf, not basketball, he could have played on the PGA Tour. The amount of practice it takes to play professional golf is as great, if not even greater, than what it takes to make the NBA, so you can't really do both.

In 2017, the Web.com Tour invited Steph to play in an event in Hayward, California, near the Warriors' arena in Oakland, even though he was just an amateur, recreational player. He did well, shooting a respectable score of seventy-four on each day. He even finished ahead of a few professional players.

Seth played many different sports, too, and found a passion for fishing. Sydel, meanwhile, followed her mom into volleyball. Dell didn't do much coaching, just small pointers. He tried to just enjoy watching his children play the sports they loved and encouraged them to be multisport athletes. Dell believed that a child didn't need to specialize in one sport until later. He thought they would benefit from learning lots of different skills and having fun. He particularly liked golfing with Steph and fishing with Seth.

Steph did play basketball, of course. He was a particularly good ball handler and shooter for his age. In elementary and middle school, he was often the smallest player on the court, but he could dribble through opponents and chuck up shots that went in. He and Seth also played relentless games in the driveway, usually with each one claiming the other fouled them and Sonya having to come out and break up arguments and fights. Neither brother wanted to give an inch. Steph, the older brother, felt he had to win. Seth, two years younger, was forever trying to prove he belonged. Little did the two brothers know they would both one day reach the NBA. That meant their family games were early training between two very talented and very competitive players.

Steph's father, Dell, is considered an easygoing personality. While he was a fierce competitor in the NBA, he was mostly quiet and happy-go-lucky off the court. It is Sonya, Steph's mother, who is known as the fiery and outspoken parent. She was a college volleyball player despite standing only five foot three. Everyone credits Dell for giving Steph his jump shot. His mom, however, deserves equal recognition for fostering his relentlessness. "I always try to claim his tenacity and his determination to never give up," Sonya once told ESPN, "to just keep working at it. Work, work, work." She also worked herself. Despite being busy with three children and a husband who was often out of town for games, Sonya founded the Christian Montessori School of Lake Norman, just north of Charlotte. She wanted to provide a faith-based school for the children of the area, including her own.

For the 1998–99 season, when Steph was ten, his father began playing for the Milwaukee Bucks, upsetting the family life. Sonya and the kids remained in Charlotte mostly and would go to Milwaukee for stretches to visit Dell. In 1999, Dell joined the Toronto Raptors, where he would play for three seasons. Initially the family remained in Charlotte and tried to continue living apart. It was tough, so Sonya moved the family to Canada for the 2001–02 season and school year. Everything changed for Steph, who would have been an eighth grader at Charlotte Christian, where he knew everyone. Instead he was the new kid in a new town in a new country.

Steph and Seth, two grades behind him, enrolled at Queensway Christian College, a tiny K-12 school in Toronto with a total enrollment of just two hundred. It was known for its strong academics, not its athletics. Each grade had only a dozen or so students, so there were no tryouts for teams. Everyone made it. Queensway Christian basketball was not very good. "We were the biggest ragtag group of people ever," Casey Field, who played on the team, told the *Toronto Star* newspaper. "We were flat-out terrible. We were not a basketball school."

Then the children of Dell Curry enrolled, and since Dell was a popular veteran on the Raptors, the students at Queensway Christian were excited to have a touch of fame and hopefully add some talent. Both Steph and Seth were so small, though, that no one was expecting much at first glance. Then on the first day of practice they started dribbling through everyone and draining shots.

The team that had been "flat-out terrible" suddenly couldn't lose. Seth played point guard and Steph played shooting guard. Playing other small schools that weren't basketball powers either, Queensway Christian began winning by thirty, forty, even fifty points a night. Teams would send three or four defenders at the Curry brothers, who then just passed it to a wide-open teammate. Their coach had to try to keep the scoring down in a display of sportsmanship. The season became a dream, and Queensway Christian won every game, including a come-from-behind victory in the championship game when Steph hit a bunch of clutch three-pointers to win the title.

"What for me stood out was that he was just a really down-to-earth, humble guy," Field said of his former teammate who became famous. "He did not have any big head about it, even though he was clearly the best player in Ontario at the time."

That winter was Dell Curry's final season in the NBA. After sixteen years he retired, and the family moved back to Charlotte, their one-year run in

Toronto complete. After a cold winter in Canada, the warmth of the American South was calling. Sonya wanted to get back to running her school. Dell looked forward to having some free time for his children. His basketball career was over. His son's career was just getting going.

3

High School

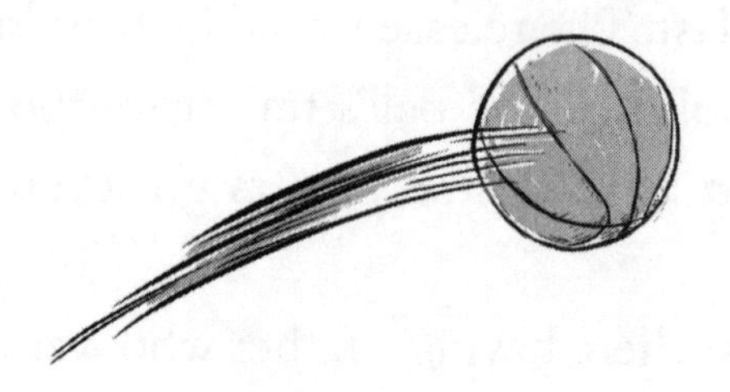

STEPH CURRY WAS a great shooter in middle school. That didn't guarantee he would be a great shooter in high school. He had to be aware of taller, stronger opponents blocking his shot. That meant he had to learn to shoot farther and farther away from the basket, and often release the shot as fast as possible before an outstretched arm could swat the ball away. To do so, he used to hold the ball on one hip and begin his shooting motion from there. Just to reach the basket, he had to put all his weight into hoisting up a jumper. His release point was usually around his shoulders. It was more of a heave than a shot. It's not uncommon for kids his age.

He could get away with that at little Queensway Christian College. Now back in North Carolina and again enrolled at Charlotte Christian, facing off against much tougher and bigger competition, it wouldn't last. The release would be too slow and the starting point of the ball's trajectory too low. He'd be easy to block as the players got even taller and faster.

Here's where having a father who was one of the greatest shooters in basketball history really helped. Dell saw Steph's weakness and agreed to help him correct it . . . if Steph was willing to put in the work needed to rebuild the shot. And not just an afternoon or two of work, Dell warned his son. Weeks and months and even years of work, something that never really ends. Even as a pro, Steph often takes a thousand practice shots in a day. Essentially, Steph would need to learn to shoot by holding the ball at his forehead and pushing from there, rather than from his hip/shoulder. It was an entirely new shot. It wouldn't be easy.

Steph said he was up to it. He had always been

the kind of person who wanted to address a problem and get better at it, usually all on his own. In this case, he'd have some help. He was also excited to have his father around every day. Now retired from the NBA, Dell no longer was spending hours each afternoon at practice or flying out of town with the team.

On the family's hoop, down at a park, or inside a gymnasium, the Currys, father and son, began to work tirelessly on reinventing Steph's shot (Seth was also often involved, too). They took all the positive aspects of Steph's game—accuracy, vision, balance, hand-eye coordination, and a sense of distance and space. Then they incorporated a new motion, the one fans see today tearing up the NBA.

But as Steph's dad had warned, the transformation didn't happen overnight. Progress was slow. Frustrations were great. Steph admits there were days, for the first time in his life, when he hated basketball. There were days, he said, when he dreaded practice. More than once the rest of the family heard Steph struggle and question out loud if it was worth it. He couldn't hit as many shots the new way as he could the old way. Dell gently pushed forward, though, challenging his son. "He wasn't like a drill sergeant," Steph said. "He was more supportive. He encouraged my work ethic. It was nice to have one of the best shooters in NBA history to help me."

Dell had grown up deep in the country, in a house a few miles outside of the little town of Grottoes, Virginia. His father, Jack, worked long hours at the local General Electric plant and farmed a large garden to help feed the family, which included Dell's four sisters. He pegged up a hoop in the yard as a way of keeping his son busy. Dell, a perfectionist at heart, took to trying to perfect his jump shot. The truth was, there wasn't much else to do. Dell was a great athlete, but living so far from other kids, he couldn't just walk over to a friend's house, a city park, or a gymnasium. He had to play alone. You can't throw a football to yourself. You *can* shoot baskets.

Many afternoons it was just Dell, a ball, and that hoop. The "court" was uneven and made of dirt, or if it rained, mud. The rim of the basket was unforgiving. You basically needed to swish the shot through or it would bounce out, hit the dirt, and dribble off into a field or the nearby woods. If you made the shot, however, the ball would drop down through the net like a feather. Dell learned his deadly accuracy and the importance of a high-arcing, soft-as-church-music shot out of necessity. He didn't want to have to chase the ball. That is what he wanted to teach his son, who had access to NBA practice facilities but needed to learn the lessons he himself had learned in a slower, simpler time out in rural Virginia.

Despite the frustrations, every day brought improvement for Steph. Learning to do it the right way was better than learning to do it the easy way. Hour after hour they practiced. Steph did even more by himself. There were times he shot a thousand jumpers in a day. "I took my form and just got as many repetitions as I could until my arms got tired and came back the next day and did the same thing," Steph said. "It's a never-ending process."

There were no cheering crowds. There were no television cameras. There was no scoreboard. Neither Dell nor Steph could even envision that this would lead to NBA stardom. They were just trying to shoot the ball the right way and get ready for high school.

"Fundamentals," Steph said. "You've got to have good balance. A lot of people focus on your hands, but it starts at your base, at your feet, being square to the basket and having good balance. You've got to have solid follow-through, each shot is smooth. I think the third thing is trying to shoot the same way every single time. And that comes with a lot of practice. Everybody has different form. You can look at every single NBA player, everybody shoots a different way. But the best shooters shoot the exact same way every time they look at the basket."

When it came time for Steph to rejoin the Charlotte Christian team and pick his jersey number, the choice was simple. Dell Curry had always worn the number 30. He wore it at Virginia Tech. He wore it in the NBA for five different teams: Utah, Cleveland, Charlotte, Milwaukee, and Toronto. Not surprisingly, his sons wore it, too, grabbing 30 in youth basketball leagues whenever they could. Both Steph and Seth wear it in the NBA. Steph's number 30 Golden State jersey is the top-selling jersey in the NBA, worn by kids and adults around the world. The number 30 is the Curry family number. You can't imagine any of them wearing anything else.

Except Steph didn't wear it at Charlotte Christian. As a freshman on the junior varsity he was told to grab a jersey. He took number 30, of course. When he slipped it on, though, it was way too big. The jerseys got bigger as the numbers got higher, and an extra-large was too much for his frame. He had to downsize. He became number 20.

Size was a challenge Steph always dealt with. It also is what sent him to the JV squad. Because of his size, he was so uncertain of himself that he didn't try out for the varsity as a freshman. To this day, he regrets that he feared failure so much he didn't try. "I wished I had pushed myself," Steph said. "That taught me a lot—to just go for it and challenge yourself in that regard and not let doubts or what people might tell you or how short or skinny you might be deter you from where you want to be."

Steph excelled his freshman year on the junior varsity. As a sophomore he was ready to shine on the varsity. And shine he did. His ball-handling skills and accurate jump shot made him a sensation. Fans flocked to games and cheered as this little kid ran circles around bigger opponents and hit shots that didn't seem possible. Charlotte Christian wasn't a big public school, but as word about Steph got out during his high school career, more and more locals with no ties to the school began flocking to the games just to watch.

No one thought Steph was the best player in North Carolina, but he may have been the most fun to watch. His court vision allowed him to make exciting passes to open teammates. There were times when he'd be on a breakaway and suddenly stop short and pull up for a three-pointer, which seems routine now when he does it for Golden State but was unheard of then. Of course, he made most of them. At least he was shooting. If anything, the biggest challenge his coach, Shonn Brown, had was making Steph realize he needed to shoot more. Steph was worried his teammates might think he was being selfish. Coach Brown assured him that in order for Charlotte Christian to win, he needed to shoot and score.

Offense wasn't the only strength of Steph's game. He was a deceptively good defensive player. He wasn't tall enough to block many shots. And he wasn't strong enough to battle on the boards for tough rebounds. His feet and hands were very quick, though. He was good at chasing down loose balls. Mostly he tried as hard on the defensive end as he did on the offensive end. The reason? His mother. She was that hard-nosed, too-small volleyball player, after all. She reinforced the importance of defense and tenacity. If Dell was known for being smooth, Sonya was known for being tough.

"My defensive aggression comes from her,"

Steph said. "She won't let me slip up. Especially in high school. She would be right there on the sidelines yelling. I can make all the shots in the world, but if I let my man score, she would be all over me after the game. I'd score thirty, and she would be like, 'You had a horrible game because you didn't play defense.' Hustling, I get all that from her."

Charlotte Christian won their conference all three years Steph was on the varsity team. All three years they advanced to the state tournament. Steph's senior year (and Seth's sophomore) was their best, reaching the North Carolina Independent Schools Athletic Association 3A Championship game before losing a heartbreaker to powerhouse Greensboro Day School. It was the end of a great high school career for Steph, where he was named all-state and became Charlotte Christian's all-time leading scorer.

They eventually retired his jersey—number 20.

But now it was time for bigger and better competition—if he could even earn a chance to play at the college level.

03.5

4

Recruitment

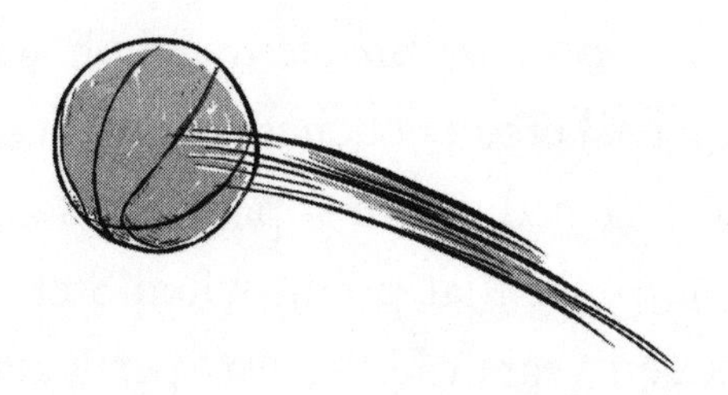

ONE AFTERNOON IN 1984, the Virginia Tech men's basketball team walked off the practice floor in Blacksburg, Virginia. Waiting for them to leave was the school's women's volleyball team. That's when Dell Curry, a junior basketball star, noticed Sonya Adams, a freshman volleyball player. Soon Dell asked Sonya to one of his games and they began dating. They got married after Dell graduated and was drafted by the Utah Jazz.

The Currys were always loyal to Virginia Tech,

rooting for the teams and talking up the school. They made return visits, dragging their three children along with them to the school's beautiful campus tucked on the edge of the Blue Ridge Mountains. Naturally, Steph wanted to go to Virginia Tech also. He wanted to be like his mom and dad and star for the Hokies.

There was one *big* problem: Steph wasn't very big. College basketball coaches tend to scout potential recruits when they are sophomores and juniors in high school. At that point, when Steph was just fifteen, sixteen years old, he was particularly small, approximately five-seven and 120 or 130 pounds.

"That's nowhere near the physical stature you need to be on that level," Steph said.

Virginia Tech was in the Atlantic Coast Conference, considered the best college basketball league in the country. It was expected to compete with powerhouses such as Duke, North Carolina, and Maryland, all of whom won national championships. When the school took a look at Curry, they saw a great shooter and talent but a thin, undersized kid who might struggle to compete against guards who were six foot three, six foot five. This was especially a concern on defense. Could Steph really guard bigger players? While Dell was six-four,

Sonya was only five-three. So while Curry was expected to grow taller and stronger, no one knew just how much taller and stronger. Would he be more like his dad, or his mom?

Virginia Tech couldn't be certain, and they weren't alone. None of the bigger schools in the area were recruiting Steph very hard. The coaches at Virginia Tech said he could come to school there, but as a freshman he would have to pay his own tuition and room and board and be a so-called walk-on player. He also wouldn't get to play that season; he would have to sit it out in what the National Collegiate Athletic Association (NCAA) calls a "redshirt year." The school would then offer him a scholarship and he could play the next four years. That wasn't really a deal that appealed to Steph, who wanted to play immediately and wanted a coach who saw him as an important part of the team. In Steph's mind, Virginia Tech really wasn't an option. Neither was any other team in the ACC, all of which valued Steph on par with Virginia Tech.

"I understood," Steph said. "It was out of my control."

That didn't mean no schools were interested, though.

One of those was Davidson College, a small

private school just a thirty-minute drive north of Charlotte. Its home gym had only 5,200 seats and rarely sold out. It was Division I, though, the highest level of competition in college basketball, and it had a coach named Bob McKillop, who was considered an excellent teacher of the game. McKillop had seen Curry play in high school and knew what kind of a shooter he was. Coach McKillop wanted him to come to Davidson.

"He did look a little frail," McKillop said. "He did look very young for his age. But he could shoot and he never backed down." What truly won McKillop over, however, was the time he scouted an Amateur Athletic Union (AAU) game where Steph played poorly.

"He had about eleven turnovers in the game I saw," McKillop said. "I had been recruiting him, so I knew how good he was. But I watched the way he responded to the turnovers. He got back on defense. He didn't try to come down the court and all of a sudden make up for the turnover by taking a crazy shot hoping that by going in, people would forget his turnover. He went to the bench and he never hung his head. He patted his teammates on the back. I saw a lot of ingredients there. He's a great talent, but he's also a great young man."

After that McKillop was determined to sign Steph Curry. Steph wouldn't have to redshirt or pay his own way. Steph was worth offering a full ride and a chance to start right away.

By then, Steph had grown weary of trying to convince people he was good enough to play for them. When you've been told you're too small your entire life, only to prove everyone wrong, you get used to the doubts. If Virginia Tech, let alone Duke and North Carolina, didn't want him, then he'd go where someone did. That meant Davidson. Besides, he liked Coach McKillop. He liked the idea of staying close to home for school. And he liked how Davidson, with just 1,700 students and a pretty campus, felt more like a family than a big university. It was like a bigger Charlotte Christian. One of the unique aspects of the school was that every student gets free laundry service. You wouldn't find that at Virginia Tech or North Carolina.

Everything fit.

"Every person has dreams and hopes of where they want to go. I definitely wanted to go to Virginia Tech growing up but once high school and reality set in, I had to think about what was best for me, and Davidson was the spot for me," Curry said. "You have to look at what's on the table. And so Virginia

Tech, they were not recruiting me heavily, and teams like Davidson were."

In the fall of 2005, he signed with Davidson. As he sprouted up to over six feet that winter and continued scoring basket after basket, plenty of bigger schools did take a second look. It was too late, though. Steph said he just tried to forget about who didn't recruit him and instead gain confidence in who did.

"I think it hurt for like a day or two," Steph said. "But once I committed to Davidson, I couldn't let that affect me. I had to look on the brighter side and say, 'hey, Davidson is a better place for me, better situation, and I have to just focus on taking the most of the opportunity that I have at Davidson.'

"I knew I had to work on my game," Steph said.

CURRY
30

5

Freshman Year

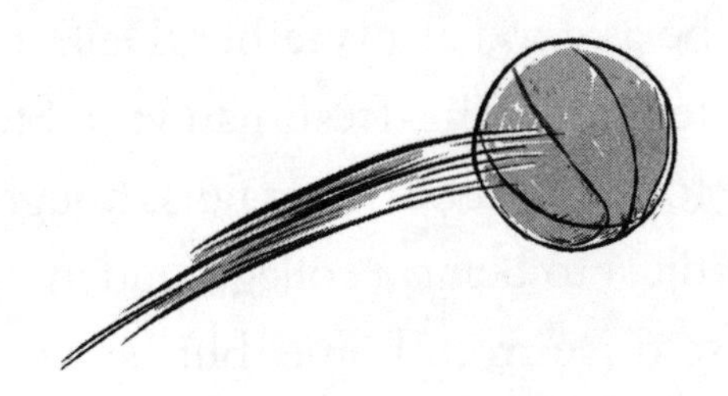

THE YEAR BEFORE STEPH joined the Davidson Wildcats, the team had gone 20–10 and earned a bid to the NCAA tournament, also known as the Big Dance or March Madness, for just the eighth time in the school's history. Though it was a Division I college, it didn't have a strong history of success like the ACC schools that had passed on Steph. America loves the tournament because it allows smaller schools such as Davidson to get a crack at bigger programs. Davidson tried hard but lost to Ohio State in the first round. With seven seniors graduating, there was a sense among fans and the media that Davidson had missed its chance to prove itself and it might take a couple of years before the Wildcats could get back to the NCAA tournament. Yes, Davidson was getting Steph Curry, but no one knew how good he would be. Could he do on the college level what he'd done at Charlotte Christian? Could he be as good as his father, Dell?

In September of his freshman year, Steph didn't have time to worry about what fans thought. He was trying to adjust to being a college student. Davidson was a close drive from home, but he was living on his own for the first time. He had to get to class by himself, study, eat, everything. There were new friends to meet and new classes to handle. It's a big adjustment for any kid.

As for basketball, the team couldn't start practice until mid-October, but right away they began playing pickup games among themselves, and Steph began to shine. "We knew he had something special," junior guard Jason Richards said. Coaches were also allowed to conduct individual instruction with players to help develop their skills. It was there that Coach McKillop realized the player he'd recruited was even better than he had thought.

Watching Steph play games was only part of the story. Everyone could see the smooth jump shot. During individual instruction, McKillop was able to see how it was formed. He'd put Steph through drill after drill—dribbling, shooting, passing, defense. Steph responded by showing not just his incredible skills but an interest in working extremely hard to get better. Everything McKillop asked him to do, Steph did to the best of his abilities. If he fell short one day, he'd be back the next trying even harder. Coach McKillop could hardly contain his excitement.

"Steph Curry, you can look at his jump shot," Coach McKillop said. "And you can look at his statistics. But what you don't see is his heart. His heart is bigger than all of those stats."

Before the season began, Coach McKillop attended a dinner in Charlotte for some of Davidson's biggest fans. They were eager for an update on the team's chances of success that season. McKillop thought they were going to be good right away. Davidson hadn't won a game in the NCAA tournament since 1969, so fans were desperate not just to make the Big Dance but to spring an upset. McKillop usually wasn't one to brag. He tended to be very conservative. He couldn't help himself this time, though.

"Wait till you see Steph Curry," McKillop told the crowd. "He is something special."

Steph had also grown. He was now over six feet tall and weighed close to 180 pounds. That was still small by college basketball standards, but it was a far cry from the little high school freshman and sophomore who McKillop had first scouted. Every day Steph lifted weights and did exercises to grow even stronger. He entered the season with big expectations. "I thought I was ready," Steph said.

Davidson's first few games were in a tournament being held in Ann Arbor, Michigan. The Wildcats played Eastern Michigan first, and then the University of Michigan after that. Michigan was a strong team out of the Big Ten, the kind of big school that people often thought was too good for Davidson. For Steph and everyone else, the chance to play Michigan was exciting, but first they had to take on Eastern Michigan.

Coach McKillop started Steph at shooting guard and expected him to not just score but also make the correct passes and help run the offense. He could shoot when he was open, but he had to protect the ball. Instead, nerves and excitement overwhelmed him. Steph kept dribbling the ball too fast, running into defenders, and making mistakes. Rather than pass to an open teammate, he threw the ball away. He couldn't settle down. He would finish the game with thirteen turnovers, way too many for any player, but especially a guard. Davidson trailed Eastern Michigan by sixteen at halftime.

In the halftime locker room, Steph wasn't sure if he was going to get benched. He wasn't playing well. He sat and wondered if maybe the critics were right. Instead Coach McKillop remained calm and reassured him that he just needed to relax and not try to do everything on every play. He reminded the team they could still win, but they had to take it one possession at a time.

The guys listened closely, and slowly Davidson began mounting a comeback, with Steph playing better in the second half. Junior Thomas Sander led the team with nineteen points, but Steph hit two three-pointers late in the game to give Davidson a lead it wouldn't surrender. They came back and won 81–77 to set up a game against Michigan the next night. Steph was just happy he'd done well. And that he'd chosen to play for Coach McKillop.

"The way Coach McKillop treated me really boosted my confidence," Steph said. "I was having my problems, but he stuck with me. If I had been taken out and left on the bench because of my poor play, I might have gotten down on myself and lost some confidence."

The next night, Steph was no longer nervous. He just wanted to prove he and his young teammates could play with Michigan. It wouldn't be easy. There were nearly nine thousand fans in Crisler Center that night, and all but a few dozen of them were rooting loudly for the Michigan Wolverines. Davidson wasn't scared, though.

They jumped out to an early lead. But Michigan proved to be the better team, winning 78–68. The story that night, though, was Steph's performance—he scored thirty-two points, grabbed nine rebounds, and, maybe most important, committed just three turnovers. The Michigan coach, Tommy Amaker, who as a player had been an All-American point guard at Duke, couldn't stop raving about Steph. "We couldn't contain him," Amaker said, shaking his head in respect. Maybe no one entered the season talking about Davidson, but they should have been. "I think their ball club is a team that will be reckoned with around the country this season," Amaker said.

Amaker was the first of many coaches to say that as Davidson began to churn out victory after victory. Davidson starters Thomas Sander and Boris Meno were great rebounders and defensive players. Will Archambault didn't start, but he had a knack for scoring quickly when he got into the game. Mostly, everyone had a job. That included Jason Richards, who became the steady point guard, which helped Steph concentrate on scoring. Davidson won twelve consecutive games at one point in the season and thirteen at another. Many of the games weren't even close. The Wildcats beat Chattanooga by thirty, Western Carolina by thirty-three, and Mount St. Mary by a whopping margin of sixty-one.

Davidson fans were ecstatic; not only was the team winning, but they were fun to watch. Steph was the star, thrilling fans who wanted to know from just how far back he could shoot three-pointers and still make them. He wasn't the entire team, though. In one game, Georgia Southern tried to shut him down by putting two or three defenders on him. Their strategy was to make someone else on Davidson beat them. That was fine with Steph's teammates. While Steph only scored four points in the first half, Jason Richards poured in twenty.

"J-Rich killed them," Curry laughed. By the time Georgia Southern switched out of that defense, it was too late. Richards finished with thirty-two and Steph with twenty-three, and Davidson won again, 101–92.

As the victories kept rolling in on the court, off the court Coach McKillop learned to appreciate Stephen's parents, especially his father. Dell was a great NBA player, so it surprised people to learn that he took a hands-off approach to his son. As far as Dell was concerned, he wasn't the Davidson coach or even Steph's coach. Bob McKillop was. That meant Steph wasn't getting mixed messages about how to play or when to shoot. "I stay out of it," Dell said. And if Steph ever got frustrated with things, his dad wasn't going to allow him to complain or take the easy way out.

"Dell Curry is the salt of the earth," Coach McKillop said. "He and his wife Sonya are the salt of the earth. They are Steph's heroes. That's a pretty special thing. Dell never, ever enters into my domain and tells me, 'You know, Steph should be doing this, Steph should be doing that.'"

It was actually the opposite. Coach McKillop and his assistants occasionally asked Dell for ideas on plays to draw up or how to get open shots. They figured his knowledge of the game could serve as a secret weapon for the Wildcats. Dell was happy to help them.

That season Steph made a point to publicly display his faith. He'd been religious his entire life, and he wanted a reminder to stay humble as he was enjoying so much success. He began writing Bible verses on his sneakers. One was Philippians 4:13, which reads: "I can do all things through Christ who strengthens me." The other was Romans 8:28: "And we know that all things work together for good to those who love God, to those who are the called according to His purpose." He scribbles those verses on his shoes to this day. Steph also developed the habit of pointing to the sky after certain parts of the game.

"I play for God and try to give Him the glory and that's my thing to take attention off myself, because it's not me, it's Him," Steph said. "He gave me the talent."

He displayed that talent in spades his freshman year, and the Wildcats won the Southern Conference regular season and tournament championships, earning a bid to the NCAA tournament. So much for fans having to wait a few years for the young players to develop!

Entering the NCAAs, Davidson was 29–4 and had gone 17–1 in the conference. Steph averaged 21.5 points a game, which ranked as the ninth highest in all of college basketball and second highest among freshmen, trailing only a guy named Kevin Durant, who played at the University of Texas and would one day become Steph's NBA teammate. Steph scored in double digits in all but one game, and his 122 three-pointers were the most made by a freshman in the history of college basketball. He was a sensation, drawing media attention with everyone wondering how the big schools ever missed recruiting him in the first place.

"We'd be pretty good if we had him," acknowledged Bill Self, the legendary head coach of the powerhouse Kansas Jayhawks, who were ranked as high as number two in the nation that year. "It is amazing. But recruiting is such an unknown science. You don't know how much guys are going to grow after they leave high school, and you don't know sometimes what they've got inside of them or the maturation process. There's always room for somebody that can really shoot and stretch the defense.

He's obviously evolved into being a terrific player."

The praise and newspaper stories were nice, but all Steph and his teammates wanted to do was win a game in the NCAA tournament. There were still critics who didn't think he'd be as good if he played in a better conference, such as the ACC. Like always, Steph had to prove the doubters wrong.

On Selection Sunday, Davidson got its wish when it was paired up against Maryland, an ACC program that had won the national title in 2002. The game was to be played in Buffalo, New York, on a neutral court so neither team would have the majority of the fans in the stands. The entire country would be watching on television to see if what they'd heard about this skinny guard from Davidson, Dell Curry's kid, was for real.

Steph proved he was. And so did Davidson. They weren't intimidated by the bigger-name team and even took an eight-point lead in the second half. In one moment of the game, Steph caught a pass on the left wing. A seven-foot Maryland player tried to guard him. Everyone in the building thought Steph would pass the ball away, but instead, as he would countless times in the years to come, he stepped back a little, created some space to shoot, and drilled a three-pointer. "Are you kidding me?" the announcer on CBS shouted. "Oh my goodness!"

Maryland closed the gap, though, and the game was hard-fought. Every time the Wildcats got ahead, the Terrapins came back. And every time Maryland got ahead, there was Steph or Jason Richards to pull Davidson back up. There were seven ties and fourteen lead changes as fans in Buffalo became enamored with Davidson.

While the crowd was supposed to be neutral, it didn't take long before everyone but those wearing Maryland colors was standing and cheering for Davidson. In the end it wasn't enough; Maryland was just a little too good, pulling away late to win 82–70. Steph scored thirty points, and when he fouled out of the game in the final minute, he received a standing ovation from the Buffalo fans, most of whom had never before seen him play. Afterward, Maryland coach Gary Williams found Steph and made sure to shake his hand and let him know that he and every other coach in the ACC had blown it by not recruiting him.

"You can play anywhere," Coach Williams told Steph.

That was of little solace for Stephen Curry and

his teammates. They wanted the win. With nearly every player returning, excitement was already building for the 2007–08 season. Maybe Davidson hadn't broken through this time, but notice had been served. There was a new power on the scene in college basketball.

6

The Big Dance

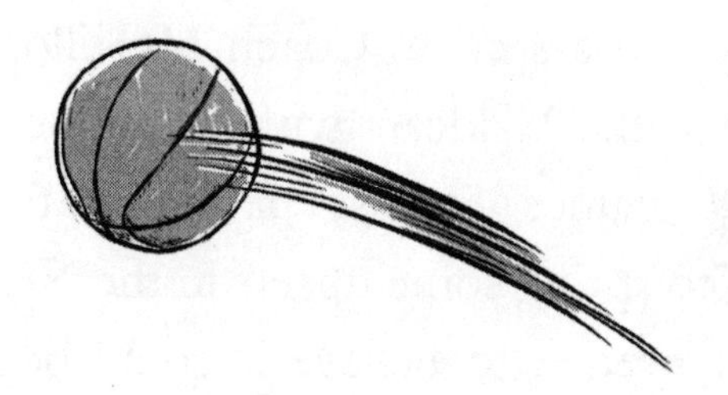

BOB MCKILLOP KNEW the 2007–08 season could be a big one. They had talent. They had experience. They had Stephen Curry. For a school the size of Davidson, such a combination doesn't come along very often. He also knew that unlike in the season before, Davidson wasn't going to sneak up on anyone. Everyone was talking about Steph. "I think the world, the basketball world, saw what Steph could do last year," Coach McKillop said.

Steph had spent the summer playing for USA

Basketball, competing in the FIBA under-19 world championships. The Americans lost to Serbia in the gold-medal game, but the opportunity helped bolster Steph's confidence since the team was filled with some of the best players who would play college basketball the following season. If he could hold his own there, he could do it anywhere.

To begin the season, Coach McKillop decided to challenge the Wildcats with a number of non-conference games against big-name teams. For Davidson to spring some upsets in the NCAA tournament, it needed to believe it could beat the big boys. McKillop scheduled games with Duke, North Carolina, North Carolina State, UCLA, and others.

It sounded like a good idea. Yet when the team started the season 3–5, there were some doubts. That was more losses than Davidson had suffered during Steph's entire freshman season. While Steph and his teammates may have been frustrated, McKillop was fine with it because even though the Wildcats were losing, they were competing. They were hanging in there with the best of the best. They lost by one to NC State, four to UNC, and six to Duke. UCLA won by eight, in part because Steph was held to just fifteen points by the Bruins point guard, whom Steph said was the best and most athletic defender he'd ever faced. That UCLA player's name? Future NBA star Russell Westbrook.

Once the Wildcats got into the Southern Conference part of the schedule, the wins came quickly. They went 20–0 in league play, steamrolling the So-Con, often in huge blowouts. They then won the Southern Conference tournament by an average of twenty-six points a game, earning an automatic bid in the NCAA tournament. The team was almost unstoppable, and it wasn't just Steph; everyone had a role. Jason Richards was now a senior point guard and he averaged 12.7 points and an incredible 8.2 assists a game.

Steph averaged 25.1 points a game, fifth most in the entire NCAA. His 162 three-pointers were the most any player had made in a season in the history of college basketball. He scored forty or more points twice, thirty or more eleven times, and twenty or more twenty-seven times. By the end of the season, nearly every sports magazine and website in the country had named him at least a second team All-American. Steph appreciated the honors but grew worried that too much attention was being paid to him. He didn't want the other players on the team to think they weren't important, too. Basketball is a team game and there is no such thing as a one-man team. At one point during the season he was asked about his secret to success.

"Our system here," Steph said. "It's nothing special that I do. I just get screens from Andrew [Lovedale] and Thomas [Sander] and other big guys down low. [Jason Richards,] our assists man, he's great at being patient and finding guys when they're open. So, when I'm open, I get the ball. I have a lot of confidence to shoot it. We've been working on our system all year, and the timing on our offense is great right now, and we're just flowing."

His teammates were thankful that their star player cared about sharing the spotlight. That doesn't always happen, especially under these circumstances. Steph was going to be an NBA player. The rest of the team were just college players, guys who would get regular jobs after graduation.

"I think he's lying," Jason Richards joked, kidding Steph about how he does "nothing special." "He gives a lot of credit to the rest of the team. That just shows what type of person he is."

With everyone on the same page and everyone

propping one another up, Davidson was a dangerous team. They entered the NCAA tournament with a 26–6 record, yet they still needed to prove themselves. Beating up on the Southern Conference and scoring lots and lots of points was one thing. Doing it against the biggest and best schools in the country was another. And if little Davidson was ever going to win an NCAA tournament game, then this had to be the year.

Ranked a tenth seed (out of sixteen in their bracket) going into the tournament, the team was sent to Raleigh, North Carolina, to face seventh-seed Gonzaga University from Spokane, Washington. Gonzaga was a strong program, making its tenth consecutive appearance in the NCAA tournament. It had twenty-five victories on the season and most experts thought they could handle Davidson.

NCAA tournament games are supposed to be held at a neutral site, but Raleigh is just a two-and-a-half-hour drive from Davidson, so the Wildcat students and fans filled the arena, seeking their first NCAA victory since 1969. The team didn't disappoint. Steph went eight of ten from three-point range as part of a monster performance, finishing with forty points, including a crucial three-pointer with a minute left to give Davidson the lead and two free throws in the final seconds to secure the 82–76 victory.

Davidson had lived up to Coach McKillop's promise and finally won an NCAA tournament game.

"It was like an opening night, a star performance on Broadway," Coach McKillop said. The victory set off wild celebrations among Davidson fans, both in the stands and back on campus. The chance to make history proved to be more meaningful for Steph than joining a college that always experiences success. Dell Curry noted that the best thing that may have ever happened to Steph was having the big schools overlook him. "Bob McKillop put him on a stage to be successful, and I don't think any other school could have done that."

As great as defeating Gonzaga was, it was still just the first round. Up next was Georgetown, a historic power from Washington, D.C. They entered the game with a 28–5 record and a reputation for tough, physical defense. And they'd done so in the Big East Conference, which had much stiffer competition than the Southern Conference.

Calm, cool, and collected Steph was not intimidated. "If we stick to our system, I think we'll be fine," he said.

That was easier said than done.

Georgetown was able to harass Steph in the first half and hold him to just five points. Every time he shot, there was a hand or two in his face. With Steph guarded so closely, his teammates struggled to get the ball into his hands. The pressure was relentless, causing fans to grow nervous that Davidson had finally found its match. Davidson trailed by seventeen points in the second half and the game seemed lost. That's when Coach McKillop gathered the team in a time-out and asked a simple question: "Are you having fun?"

The players couldn't believe it. Fun? They were losing. By a lot.

Then they realized the point. If they got back to having fun, maybe it would all come together. "We got to smiling a little bit," Jason Richards said. Just stick with the system, McKillop reminded them.

With the team's attitude adjustment, Steph was able to find some room to shoot. His teammates set hard picks and once he got an inch of daylight, he'd fire off a shot, no matter how far behind the three-point line he was. Most of those shots sailed through the net.

He scored twenty-five points in the second half to finish with thirty for the game, and

Davidson stormed back to win 74–70. It was one of the greatest comebacks in NCAA tournament history. It is one thing for a school like Davidson to win one game in the NCAA tournament. But two? Now they were cooking.

When the team bus pulled back onto campus there was a crowd of about five hundred people waiting to cheer. Everyone was suddenly a Davidson fan. Steph was the star of the NCAA tournament, and his teammates were along for the ride. Thomas Sander, for instance, was filling the tank of his car a day after the Georgetown victory, when all the other customers at the gas station gave him a standing ovation.

Steph kept trying to remind everyone that the Wildcats weren't finished and they would continue to take every day, every practice, and every game the same way. He believed in consistency and routine, the same as ever, no matter how many ESPN and CBS cameras were following them around.

Up next was the Sweet Sixteen in Detroit, Michigan, where the game would be played at Ford Field, which usually hosts the NFL's Detroit Lions. A basketball court was constructed on top of the field. A crowd of almost sixty thousand was expected, by far the biggest any Davidson player (or nearly any basketball player in the world) had ever played in front of before! Even NBA arenas rarely hold more than twenty thousand fans, and the Wildcats home court held just over five thousand.

Davidson's opponent was Wisconsin, an excellent club that had won the highly competitive Big Ten Conference and carried a 31–4 record into the game. Wisconsin had the nation's number one ranked defense, holding opponents to just 53.9 points a game. Throughout the game they tried to bang and knock Davidson players around, especially Steph. It didn't work. Steph scored thirty-three points, and Davidson blew the game open in the second half, winning 73–56. "We weren't going to back down," Steph said of the physical play.

By this point, almost everyone was sold on Davidson. They'd become America's team. That included a famous face in the huge crowd at Ford Field that night . . . LeBron James, then a twenty-three-year-old megastar for the Cleveland Cavaliers. Since the Cavs were playing an away game against the Detroit Pistons the next night, LeBron called the Davidson athletic department and asked for a couple of tickets to the game. Why sit in a hotel room and watch it on TV when you can go in person? "He's a very, very, very, very, very good basketball player," James had told reporters earlier in the week when asked about Steph. LeBron wanted to witness his game in person.

"I'm here to watch the kid," LeBron said that night to the *Cleveland Plain Dealer* newspaper.

What he saw was "the kid" put on an incredible show. Steph draining deep three-pointers. Steph coming off screens. Steph making steals. And eventually, Steph hitting a scoop reverse layup while being fouled that was so impressive, even LeBron leaped out of his seat and cheered. "It's just really cool to have a guy like LeBron James, one of the best players in the NBA right now, coming out and supporting Davidson," Steph said.

After the game Steph didn't want to spend too much time focusing on LeBron's appearance in the stands or any of the other excitement that was now surrounding him. His teammates had nicknamed him "Prime Time" that year because he always delivered in the biggest moments. Yet they were impressed that he never acted like the star. He was just another guy on the team. When Steph was named a finalist for the Wooden Award, which goes to the best college basketball player in the country, his teammates found out by watching ESPN. It was an incredible honor, but Steph never mentioned it to them, let alone bragged about it. He said he didn't think it was important.

"It's just amazing to be able to be around a great basketball player that's, at the same time, a friend and a great guy," teammate Max Paulhus Gosselin said.

The more pressing issue was playing Kansas University two days later in the Elite Eight. The winner would go to the Final Four, the biggest stage in all of college basketball, and be just two victories away from a national championship. Schools like Davidson rarely made the Final Four and never won it all. Schools like Davidson rarely have a player as good as Stephen Curry, though. Still, this would be their greatest challenge.

Kansas would finish the season 37–3. The Jayhawks were the favorite to win the national championship. They entered the game having beaten opponents by an average of over twenty points a game. They were loaded with talent. Six KU players would be selected in the NBA draft that spring. Their coach, Bill Self, was considered one of the best in America. His game plan was different than most of the other coaches' plans. He saw that having one great defender try to cover Steph didn't work. They eventually got tired chasing him around. Once that happened, Steph poured in the points in the second half. With so many talented players, Coach Self divided up the job, assigning four different Jayhawks to take turns on Steph in an attempt to wear *him* down instead.

It was a smart idea. Steph had his worst shooting performance in the NCAAs, just nine for twenty-five as he kept dealing with fresh-legged defenders. He still scored twenty-five points, and his teammates proved this was anything but a one-man team. The Wildcats played incredible defense, forcing turnovers and bad shots and keeping the game low-scoring. "They muddied the game up for us," Coach Self said. It came down to the final possession, Kansas leading by two, 59–57. Davidson had the ball with 16.8 seconds remaining. One last shot at making the Final Four.

Steph took the inbound pass and brought it up court. Kansas had decided to play "small" by putting four guards on the court to keep up with Steph. He dribbled left through a screen but ran into two Kansas defenders. He dribbled right and found two more. With time running out, he pump-faked and tried to find space for a shot but couldn't. He finally made a last-second pass to Jason Richards, who at the buzzer sent up a three-pointer.

In the stands, red-clad Davidson fans lifted their arms, hoping it would fall. On the bench, Coach McKillop looked on to see if this miracle run would continue.

Thump.

It hit off the rim and backboard and fell to the side. The buzzer sounded. Kansas won.

The Davidson Wildcats run was over, so close to the Final Four. The players fell to the floor in exhaustion. Steph chewed on his mouth guard. Kansas players came over to congratulate them on a hard-fought game. "He's a fabulous player," Coach Self said about Steph. Praise like that was nice, but not in the moment. The dream was done.

"It's going to hurt," Steph predicted. "This game's going to hurt a lot for the next however long. But I'm just happy to be a part of this team and to be a part of what we accomplished. I'm definitely proud of our team. We proved a lot of people wrong."

Kansas would go on to win the national championship. Davidson was beat, by a single basket by the best team in America.

02.4
CURRY
30

7
NBA Draft

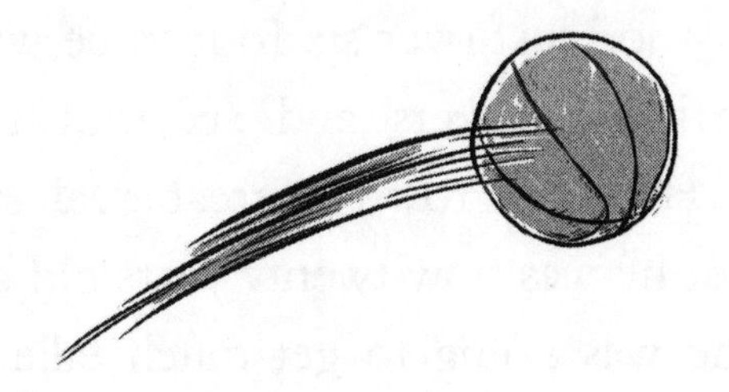

STEPH WAS ONLY a sophomore in college, but as he thrilled the nation throughout the 2008 NCAA tournament, fans and the media wondered if he was going to leave Davidson and declare himself eligible for the NBA draft. That included no less than LeBron James, who assured reporters that Steph was good enough for the NBA right now: "I don't know if he's coming out [in the draft] this year. When he does, he has a spot."

Steph saw it differently. He was certain that if

he decided to enter the NBA, he would get drafted and make a team. That wasn't his ultimate goal, however. He took a longer view. He didn't just want to make the NBA, he wanted to be great in the NBA. No matter how many shots he'd hit during his sophomore year, he didn't think he was ready for professional basketball.

Steph stood just over six foot three when wearing basketball sneakers and six foot two when barefoot. He had grown a great deal since high school, but he was now twenty years old and it was unlikely he was going to get much taller. Despite weight training and attempts to add muscle, he was still a slight 180 pounds. He was going to get only so big. And Steph and his father, Dell, believed he should get only so big. While spending hours and hours lifting weights might add bulk and muscle, it could also ruin his game.

Steph had long ago learned to use his slight build as an asset, taking advantage of the fact that he was quick, athletic, and very fluid. He could catch a pass and release his shot in less time than most other players, preventing taller, stronger defenders from blocking it. He had also learned ways to maneuver around opponents and take shots they weren't expecting. Even that famous scoop reverse layup that LeBron cheered during the NCAA tournament was something he'd developed. "I was always short growing up, so I had to figure out a way to get to the basket," Steph explained. He was who he was. It was working.

At his size, though, the Currys believed Steph would have to play point guard in the NBA. That was the position players his height typically played. Shooting guards or wing players could get as tall as six foot seven or even six foot nine. Defending them would be very difficult. Steph had terrific dribbling skills honed over the years—everyone could see that—but playing point guard requires more than that. You have to learn how to run an offense, almost like the quarterback of a football team. You have to know when and where to pass the ball, how to set others up for easy shots, and when to just shoot it yourself. His first two years at Davidson, Steph played shooting guard. Jason Richards was the point guard, and he was a great one, leading the country in assists in 2007–08 with 8.14 per game. Many of those came from passing the ball to Steph, who drained a basket.

With Richards graduating, Steph would become

Davidson's starting point guard his junior year. He saw that as a golden opportunity to gain valuable experience. He would still be expected to score, but this was almost like an internship that would help him become a great NBA player, not just an NBA player.

He knew from his father that the NBA was a business, but college basketball was more just a game to be played with his buddies. And he loved everything about Davidson and wanted one more year to be a college kid. He loved living in the dorms. He loved being so close to his family, sneaking off to play golf with his dad or going home to get a meal cooked by his mom. He loved his friends who were just regular students, not basketball players. He loved how when he was on campus, he felt he knew everyone and everyone knew him. He loved how he could just be Steph from Charlotte, not "Prime Time," not the star of the NCAA tournament, not someone who texted with LeBron.

Steph and his teammates, for example, formed an intramural softball team. When he had a free minute, he liked being a Davidson fan, regularly showing up at soccer games. He made cameos in a sketch comedy campus television program called *The Davidson Show* that got posted on YouTube.

That offseason, he would attend the ESPYs in Los Angeles and appear on *Late Night with Conan O'Brien* in New York. Yet he truly wanted to be a regular guy for as long as possible, so he did things such as volunteer to work freshman orientation, where he helped carry the bags and refrigerators of starstruck new students up to their dorm rooms.

That summer, when Steph attended the ESPYs, he used his time in Los Angeles to reconnect with a friend he knew from Charlotte. He had met Ayesha Alexander in 2002, at a youth Bible study at the Central Church of God. This was in junior high, and while they liked each other, their communication was limited to a few phone calls here or there. When Ayesha graduated from high school a year ahead of Steph, she moved to Los Angeles to pursue a career in acting. Now that he was in her town for a couple of days, Steph looked her up on social media and made a connection. Ayesha showed Steph around Hollywood, and it was clear they were going to be more than friends. That fall, Ayesha moved back to Charlotte and she and Steph were never again apart.

As for basketball, with so many seniors graduating, there was no guarantee the Wildcats would be contenders like the previous year's squad. Even if they were, the magical run would be difficult to duplicate. McKillop also loaded up the schedule with major opponents to test the Wildcats. He figured lots of nationally televised games would help with recruiting once Steph did leave for the NBA. They'd play Duke, Oklahoma, NC State, West Virginia, Purdue, and others. That was all fine with Steph. He was up for the challenge.

That summer he worked out individually on his ball-handling skills and then used his newfound fame to serve as a counselor at the summer camps of NBA players Chris Paul, Paul Pierce, and, of course, LeBron James. After the camp was done for the day, top college and NBA players competed in pick-up games. The chance to learn the point guard position from Chris Paul was a great opportunity. Paul grew up in Winston-Salem, North Carolina, starred at Wake Forest, and by then was considered one of the best at the position in the NBA.

Steph also learned something about NBA intensity. Even in late-night, informal games, the best players still played the hardest. That was particularly true of LeBron, who didn't see this as just a fun way to stay in shape, but a chance to remind everyone he was the best player in the world at the time. He played "like everyone playing against him was trying to take his job," Steph said. "He was as competitive and determined as ever."

Once the season started, Steph was no less ruthless. He scored forty-four in a loss to Oklahoma and forty-four more in a victory over North Carolina State, with LeBron again watching and cheering courtside because the Cavaliers were going to play the Charlotte Bobcats (now known as the Hornets) that evening. LeBron said he wasn't just a basketball player but a basketball fan and he'd become enamored with watching Steph.

"I saw a kid who didn't care how big someone was, how fast someone else was, how strong someone else was," James told reporters. "He just went out and played. He wasn't going to let anything when it comes to sizes, power, strength, speed, stop him from what he was able to do. It was great to see someone like that."

That was Steph. He scored forty or more four times that season and thirty or more fifteen times, all while trying to pass the ball more often as the point guard. He averaged an incredible 28.6 points per game to lead the entire country in scoring. He also recorded 5.6 assists per game compared to 2.9 the previous year, a testament to his growth as the leader of the team's offense. He was named first team All-American. Davidson wasn't quite the same team that year, however. They finished 27–8 but lost in the Southern Conference tournament and failed to make the NCAAs. There would be no March Madness rerun for Steph and the Wildcats. At the end of his junior season, with a year's experience playing point guard, Steph believed he was now ready for the challenge of the NBA. As much as he would miss Davidson, his teammates, and Coach McKillop, it was time. He formally declared himself eligible for the 2009 draft. He left Davidson as the school's greatest player, amassing 2,635 points, hitting 414 three-pointers, and averaging 25.3 points a game. But for all of his individual achievements, he'll tell you his proudest accomplishment is the eighty-five games the team won.

Those were amazing college accomplishments. No one doubted that Steph was an incredible college player anymore. Yet just like when he'd made the transition from high school to the NCAA, there were again questions about how good he could be at the next level. Was he big enough for the NBA? Was he strong enough for the NBA? Was he athletic enough for the NBA? Was he really a point guard?

The predraft scouting report on NBA.com put it this way: "Some people worry that he lacks the size, strength, and explosive athleticism to be a great NBA player. They also worry that Curry won't be able to make the transition to the pros. He's extremely small for the NBA shooting guard position, and it will likely keep him from being much of a defender at the next level. Although he played point guard his junior year, he's not a natural point guard that an NBA team can rely on to run a team. Curry is not a great finisher around the basket due to his size and physical attributes and he needs to add some muscle to his upper body."

Steph shrugged off all the criticism. It was the same old story. Players such as Blake Griffin of the University of Oklahoma and James Harden of Arizona State were considered the top picks in the 2009 draft. Steph knew he would be in the next group. Some teams didn't even consider him among the best point guards in the draft, ranking Tyreke Evans of the University of Memphis, Ricky Rubio of Spain, and Jonny Flynn of Syracuse University higher than him.

Whatever. As long as he went somewhere, Steph would be happy. And as always, he was determined to prove the naysayers wrong.

One team in particular, however, had its sights set on Steph.

Golden State had the seventh overall pick, and they said they wanted Steph. The Warriors general manager at the time, Larry Riley, had spent years scouting him. It wasn't just Steph's game that made Riley certain he was going to be a star. It was the way he worked in practice. Riley believed Steph would continue to improve once he got to the NBA.

The problem for the Currys was that Golden State almost never had a good team. And this current squad certainly wasn't. It went just 29–53. They also had a player a lot like Steph, Monta Ellis, a six-foot-three guard who averaged 19.0 points a game. Then there was Stephen Jackson, who at six foot eight played shooting guard and averaged 20.7 points a game. The Currys were concerned that Steph would be stuck without a clear position on a team that lost often. When Golden State tried to bring him in to work out for them, the Currys declined. They hoped the Warriors would lose interest and draft someone else and he would fall either to the New York Knicks at number eight or the hometown Charlotte Hornets, Dell's old team, at number twelve.

The NBA draft doesn't offer a choice to the

players, however. If you get picked, you get picked, so when the family arrived at the draft that night, they just celebrated that he was going to go somewhere. Sonya Curry brought a small sign that read THANK YOU DAVIDSON to flash for the ESPN cameras. "Just remembering where I came from [and] my teammates," Steph said. "That was just a way of saying 'hi' to the community back there that meant so much to me." When his name was finally called to become a member of the Golden State Warriors as the seventh overall pick in the 2009 NBA draft, Steph briefly bowed his head and said a quick prayer to God. "Just a little way of thanking him for this opportunity," Steph said. He may have wanted New York or Charlotte, but he vowed to do everything he could to succeed with the Warriors.

He soon hugged his father, who was celebrating his forty-fifth birthday; his mother; his sister, Sydel; and, of course, Ayesha. Then he went and hugged NBA commissioner David Stern. He was officially in the NBA.

Now the question was: What was he going to do with the opportunity?

02.3

02.2

02.1

8

Welcome to Golden State

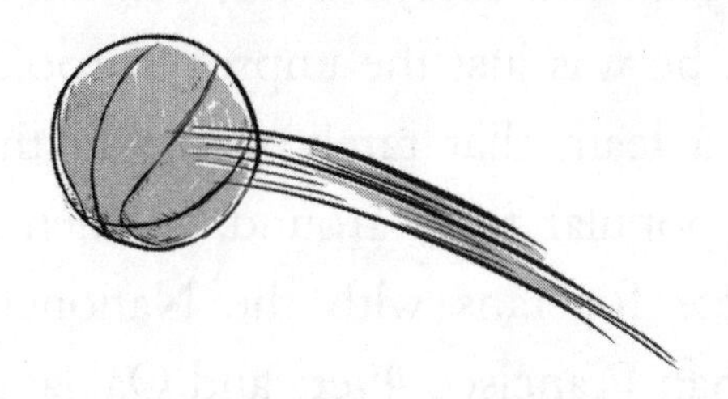

THE SAN FRANCISCO BAY AREA is a long way from Charlotte, North Carolina, or tiny Davidson College. It is one of the biggest, most exciting, and most diverse places in the entire world. Seven million people live there.

San Francisco is a bustling, hilly city with lots of culture and a view of the Golden Gate Bridge. Oakland, which is home to Oracle Arena, where Golden State plays, sits just across the bay and is known for hard work and industry. To the south of both cities is San Jose and Silicon Valley, home to major tech companies such as Google, Apple, and Facebook. Each city is a little different. All together, they make up the Bay Area, Steph Curry's new home.

For Steph, it was an exciting time for him and Ayesha, who was now his girlfriend. Charlotte is more of a midsize city, and at Davidson he knew almost everyone on campus from professors to new students. And everyone knew him. Now in the Bay Area, he was just the unproven rookie for the Warriors, a team that rarely won and thus wasn't the most popular team around. Golden State had to compete for fans with the National Football League's San Francisco 49ers and Oakland Raiders, Major League Baseball's San Francisco Giants and Oakland Athletics, the National Hockey League's San Jose Sharks, plus the college teams at Stanford and the University of California, Berkeley. Few games at Oracle were even sold out.

The positive for Steph was that he no longer lived in a fishbowl. He and Ayesha liked to think of themselves not as stars or celebrities but regular people with very interesting jobs. Steph appreciated that he could slip on a baseball cap and go explore the city. Almost no one looked twice at them. They were just another young couple walking around, getting coffee, touring a museum, or going out to dinner. They got to know the Bay Area on their own. They were another pair of young people who moved to the city for a new job.

As for basketball, Steph knew that just making the NBA meant nothing. He knew from hanging around his dad's NBA locker rooms as a kid that players who were on the team one day were off it the next. Being a professional basketball player is a dream job. It's exciting and fun. Only the best players enjoy stability, though. Everyone else is just trying to keep their spot on the team. Each NBA team has thirteen active players on its roster. There are thirty teams, meaning there are only 390 NBA players, with guys all over the world hungry to take their jobs.

Steph was determined to last, like Dell did for sixteen seasons. Even as a "lottery pick," or one of the first fourteen players selected overall, very little was guaranteed. While the Warriors believed in him, others wondered about his chances of success, especially with Monta Ellis, who had a similar game and was a fan favorite, already starting.

Don Nelson was the coach of the Warriors when Steph joined the team. As a player, Nelson won five NBA championships with the Boston Celtics before becoming a coach. He was a three-time NBA coach of the year and was known as an innovator. He believed in so-called "small ball," where a team would play three guards and try to run and gun to victory. It was successful, and his teams often won many games, but they usually fell short in the playoffs.

Steph spent his rookie season trying to prove he could be an NBA point guard. While he made strides at the position, he often forced passes and turned down jump shots he could have made to set up other players. He averaged 17.5 points a game but took fewer than five three-pointers a game. As for turnovers, which had been a problem for him in college, he averaged 3.0 a game against just 5.9 assists. It was too low of a ratio for a point guard. The team never gelled. They finished with a record of 26–56, nowhere near the playoffs. It was the same old Warriors. Just before the start of the 2010–11 season, Golden State decided to replace Don Nelson.

His assistant, Keith Smart, was hired as an interim coach for the season. Coach Smart was not the best fit for Steph. First, he wanted a more traditional point guard, one who would look to pass first and deliver a high assist-to-turnover ratio. That wasn't Steph, whose game was so free-flowing it led to mistakes. You had to take the bad with the great. At that stage of his career, Steph also struggled because he was trying too hard to be a pure point guard, forcing passes sometimes or looking too much at setting up others. It seemed anytime Steph made a bad pass or a bad decision, Coach Smart would pull him from the game. Steph averaged just 14.2 shots a game that season, and just 4.6 three-pointers. His scoring average ticked up to 18.6 points a game, but the Warriors were only slightly better than the previous season, finishing with a 36–46 record.

For Steph, the highlight of the season came at the NBA all-star game, when he competed in the Skills Challenge. It's a contest to judge shooting, ball handling, and passing. It's a timed event where each player races through a series of challenges. That year you had to hit a layup, dribble around four obstacles, make a chest pass through a tire target, then a bounce pass through another, hit a top-of-the-key jumper, make a longer pass through a hoop, then dribble back down the court through four obstacles and in for a dunk or layup. The other competitors were Chris Paul, Russell Westbrook, Derrick Rose, and John Wall. The event is purely for fun, but for Steph, it was a chance to prove he belonged with those guys, some of the best young stars in the league. Steph wound up winning with a time of 28.2 seconds, beating Westbrook in the finals. It was a nice victory but a bittersweet one. The goal of the all-star weekend was to play in the actual all-star game. He was still a long way from being considered that type of player.

Earlier that same season, in December 2010, in a game against San Antonio, Steph had rolled his right ankle while trying to change directions with the ball. It was sprained and he hobbled off the court. Injuries happen in the NBA, but this was a strange one. Usually NBA-caliber athletes don't just sprain an ankle without stepping on someone else's foot or landing awkwardly. Steph struggled with the ankle all season, missing six games and having to limit his playing time in others after various tweaks. It was a sign of problems to come.

That off-season, Steph had surgery to reattach

some torn ligaments in his ankle. The hope was that it would strengthen with rehab and be fine. Steph had never had a problem with his ankle in high school or college, so he hoped this would be no big deal. The rehab, though, held back his off-season training regimen. He knew he needed to get better, and the off-season is when players are really able to concentrate on their own games and not worry about the team.

As if that wasn't enough turmoil for one off-season, Golden State announced they would not retain Coach Smart as the team's head coach. Instead they hired Mark Jackson, a former NBA point guard who was working as a broadcaster for ESPN before being hired by the Warriors.

Steph had high hopes for his third season, 2011–12. Unfortunately, it proved to be a nightmare. In January, he sprained his ankle again and missed two weeks recovering. Everyone was nervous. Had the surgery not worked? Or was this just a fluke? Then on March 10, 2012, in a game against Dallas, he rolled the ankle again, limped to the bench, and in frustration punched his seat. At the time, he didn't think it was serious. A trainer taped it up tight and Steph asked to go back in the game.

It turned out to be worse than he imagined.

First the team decided to sit him for two weeks, then two more. Finally, by late April, with Golden State on its way to another disappointing year, doctors and coaches determined Steph needed another surgery. He had played just twenty-six games in his third NBA season and was developing a reputation for being injury-prone—which fed into the belief that he was too small and slight to even play in the league.

Steph was frustrated. The next surgery made him nervous. When he went to the hospital in Los Angeles, the plan called for doctors to remove the tendon in his right ankle and replace it with a tendon from a dead body. That sounded weird. However, when doctors sent a small camera into his ankle to see the issue, they were pleasantly surprised. The tendon was damaged but didn't need to be replaced. They cleaned up some scar tissue and quickly ended the surgery. The dead-body tendon wasn't needed and would go to someone else. More rehab was the answer. Steph was pleased but concerned. Would the injuries ever end? Could he really make it in the NBA?

As his third season in the league ended, he no more had the answer to that than he did when he left Davidson.

01.9
30
30
01.7
CURRY
30
30
1.5

9

Rising Up

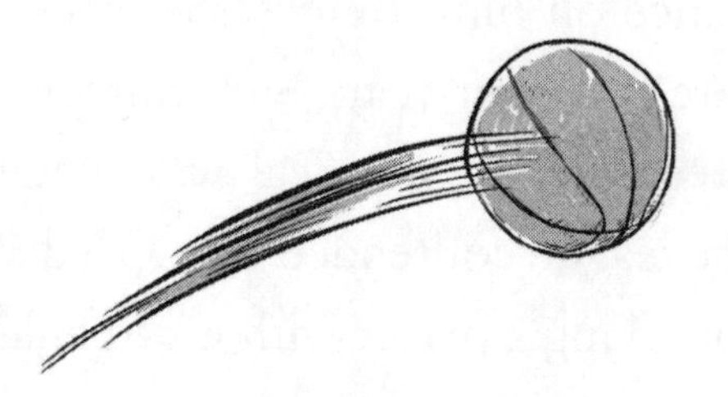

IN THE NBA, young players make a lot of money. Steph's first contract paid him $2,710,560 as a rookie, $2,913,840 for his second year, and $3,117,120 for his third. That's a lot of cash, and Steph appreciated every penny of it. Veteran players, though, especially stars, make a lot more than that. At the start of the 2012–13 season, Steph was entering his fourth and final year of his first contract. It called for him to be paid $3,958,742. That same year, Kobe Bryant of the Los Angeles Lakers was going to make $27.9 million!

An NBA player's so-called second contract is when his pay goes up. Due to his ankle injuries, however, Steph was now viewed as a risky bet. Signing him to a big-money contract when no one knew if he could even play long-term, let alone how good he could become, was dangerous.

Thankfully for Steph, Golden State decided to take a chance on him. Before the 2012–13 season, they offered a four-year, $44 million extension. Steph agreed. When the deal was made, whispers around the league contended that Golden State was foolish for giving a player with a bad ankle so much cash.

In the long run, it would turn out to be one of the best bargains in NBA history.

Steph felt good going into the season. His rehab work had been grueling but effective. He worked with trainers, and it was determined that Steph shouldn't just spend time strengthening his ankle but also his entire lower body in an effort to prevent future injuries. They began a regimen that included lifting and stretching his entire leg, his glutes, and even his abs. Steph also polished his footwork and tried to concentrate on the way he ran and cut in an effort to spare a pounding on his ankles. It was boring and repetitive, but by the start of the season, he was holding up well physically.

The Warriors were changing also. Late in the previous season, the team had traded Monta Ellis to Milwaukee in exchange for seven-foot center Andrew Bogut, the kind of big man they needed. That meant Steph would be the primary perimeter scorer. The roster was filling out in other places, too.

In 2011, the team had drafted a six-foot-seven shooting guard named Klay Thompson, who had been impressive in his rookie season. Klay was similar to Steph in a lot of ways. His father, Mychal, had played thirteen seasons in the NBA and won two titles with the Lakers. His mother, Julie, was also a college volleyball player. As a high schooler, Klay, like Steph, was not heavily recruited. Even though he played high school basketball in the Los Angeles area, neither UCLA nor USC were interested in Klay. Major college coaches worried about his defense and thought he was too skinny to be a big-time player.

The only school in the Pac-12 Conference, which comprises many of the major basketball schools in the west, to offer him a scholarship was Washington State, which sits in rural eastern Washington and rarely reaches the NCAA tournament. Klay accepted it and, like Steph did at Davidson, used the doubters as motivation to get better while appreciating the coaching staff who did believe in him. Over his three years at Washington State, Klay was named all-conference twice, averaged 21.6 points a game as a junior, and became an NBA lottery pick. He made a lot of West Coast coaches look foolish. Now he and Steph, two guys who hadn't received much attention from major college programs out of high school, were the future of the Golden State Warriors.

That off-season, the Warriors also made two other smart draft picks. They chose small forward Harrison Barnes from the University of North Carolina in the first round. He was considered an excellent offensive player. In the second round, they took a shot at a tough but undersized power forward out of Michigan State named Draymond Green. Where other teams saw limits in what Green could do, the Warriors saw a guy who was a terrific rebounder, excelled on defense, and could play multiple positions and would keep working to get better. With Steph and Klay shooting from the outside and Andrew Bogut on the inside, scoring wasn't going to be an issue. They thought Draymond would be perfect.

The effect of all this new talent on the roster was immediate. The 2012–13 season was Golden State's best in years. The Warriors went 47–35 and finished second in the Pacific Division behind the Los Angeles Clippers. Steph's ankle held up, and he missed just four games and only had a few minor setbacks. Mostly, though, he excelled as the team's main offensive threat. He averaged a career-high 22.9 points a game. Klay added 16.6 points a game as a full-time starter. The Warriors reached the playoffs for the first time since 2007 and only the second time since 1994. Once there, they defeated Denver in the opening-round best-of-seven series, 4–2, before losing to San Antonio in the following best-of-seven round, 4–2.

Crowds began returning to Oracle Arena as Bay Area basketball fans grew to love the team. For Steph, it was a season where he finally proved to himself, if not to the rest of the league, just how good he could be. And with the off-season to get better, not just rehab his ankle, he thought the sky was the limit.

"I think I've kind of given myself an idea of

what I'm capable of as a player when I'm healthy," Steph said at the time. "Hopefully ankle troubles are completely behind me. This will be the first summer I'll be able to work on my game since my rookie year, so I'm excited about the possibilities of adding things to my skill set."

That season, Steph and Klay had begun to feel comfortable playing together. They were comfortable taking three-point shots whenever open. They also sensed when one or the other was *feeling it* and ready to fire shots at will. If Klay was making shots, Steph passed to him. If Steph was on, Klay sent it back. Steph would hit 272 shots from behind the arc that season, breaking the NBA record at the time, just a few more than the 269 Ray Allen, then of the Boston Celtics, had made in 2005–06. Klay, meanwhile, would hit 211 three-pointers. Their combined 483 was the most ever by two teammates. Coach Jackson declared them "the greatest shooting backcourt in the history of the game."

One of the most memorable moments of the season came in December, when the Warriors were playing the Charlotte Bobcats. Steph and Klay were particularly hot, combining to hit seven of eleven three-pointers in the first half of an eventual easy Warriors victory. During halftime, Brian Witt, a writer for Warriors.com, tweeted out the pair's impressive stats and added a hashtag: #SplashBrothers. At the time, he didn't think much of it. It was a play on a nickname given to two great former Oakland Athletics baseball players, Jose Canseco and Mark McGwire, best known for hitting lots of home runs. They were called the "Bash Brothers." The "Splash Brothers" nickname took off instantly on social media. It was perfect, not just for how many three-pointers Steph and Klay made, but for the way their high-arcing shots seemed to splash into the net. Soon it was how everyone was referring to this young, exciting Golden State backcourt.

"It's a pretty accurate term, I'd like to say," Steph said. "I don't think we've called each other that ever, but it's fun."

As much as 2012–13 felt like a breakout season for Steph, not everyone was convinced. Coming into the NBA, he had signed an endorsement contract with Nike. He wasn't one of the company's main stars, like LeBron, Kobe Bryant, or, of course, Michael Jordan. Still, Nike liked to sign a lot of good young talent in case one of them developed into a big-time player. Whereas Nike originally considered Steph a possible star, when his contract ended after the season, it didn't work hard to re-sign him. Instead, Nike's approach was lukewarm.

They didn't offer him much money. They didn't put a big plan in place for how to use him. Steph felt shunned. Here he was again, still doubted. Fortunately for him, Under Armour was trying to make a bigger push in basketball, and they saw something blossoming. They pursued Steph hard, and like when Davidson offered him out of high school, Steph felt he should go where he was most wanted. Nike told him he was making a mistake. He didn't care. He was now an Under Armour player.

The Splash Brothers continued to dominate in the 2013–14 season. They combined to break their own teammate three-point record, hitting 484 together. Steph made 261 of them and averaged 24.0 points a game. Klay hit 223 and averaged 18.4 points. For a third consecutive year Steph competed in the three-point contest (he fell short again), but the real highlight was that fans voted him in as a starter for the actual all-star game. His 1,047,281 votes were the most for any guard in the league and second among all players in the Western Conference, behind only Oklahoma City's Kevin Durant.

"To not only be here, but starting is definitely a dream come true," Steph said.

The Warriors had another strong season, going 51–31. The arrival of veteran forward Andre Iguodala from the Denver Nuggets helped add a strong defender and all-around player. Golden State was better than ever, although it didn't show in the playoffs, where they lost a hard-fought opening-round series to the Clippers, 4–3. Soon after the loss, the Warriors owners, Joe Lacob and Peter Gruber, surprised the team by firing Coach Jackson, even though he'd delivered the best two-year run the team had enjoyed in years.

There were many reasons to fire Mark Jackson, but one of them was a belief that the team could play better under a new coach, namely Steve Kerr. Coach Kerr had once been a great player, a star at the University of Arizona before playing fifteen seasons in the NBA. He was a shooting guard, and although he never averaged double-digit points, he was known for hitting jump shots in the most pressurized moments of a game. He played mostly for the Chicago Bulls and the San Antonio Spurs, where he combined to win five NBA championships. He also got to be a teammate of some of the greatest players in history, including Michael Jordan and Scottie Pippen in Chicago and Tim Duncan, David Robinson, Manu Ginobili, and Tony Parker in San Antonio.

Kerr's most memorable highlight came in Game 6 of the 1997 NBA Finals, right when the Bulls needed a basket to win the championship. A double-teamed Michael Jordan passed him the ball with just seconds remaining. Kerr stepped up and hit a seventeen-footer, and Chicago won the title.

Kerr was known as a smart player. Being around so many Hall of Fame talents taught him a great deal about how championship teams work in the NBA. In addition, he played for two of the greatest coaches of all time, eleven-time NBA champion Phil Jackson in Chicago and five-time NBA champion Gregg Popovich in San Antonio. He spent many years as a broadcaster for TNT, traveling around the league calling games and meeting with coaches and players. He would pick their brains about different styles of play and how to motivate teams. While many thought he was just preparing for that night's broadcast, he was actually preparing to become a coach himself.

Even though Steve Kerr had never before

coached a team, Golden State thought he was the ideal choice to take an exciting young roster, apply an innovative offense, and turn the Warriors from a team that just reached the playoffs into one that could win championships. And Kerr, who was also offered the chance to coach the New York Knicks, decided that Golden State was the perfect place for him. He saw a champion in the making, too.

"The greatest moments of my career have come through team-building, being on championship teams," Kerr said. "It's the magic that occurs when a group of players, coaches, and management can come together and achieve something. I've been preparing. I've put together a philosophy, a plan. This is something I've thought about for a long time."

Steve Kerr had a plan that would not only change the career of Steph Curry and the direction of the Golden State Warriors, but one that would change the NBA.

01.2

10

Champions

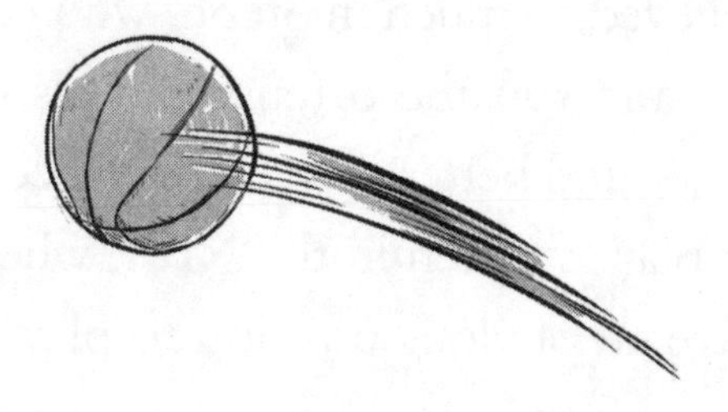

BEFORE STEVE KERR was hired to shake things up, in 2011, Bob Myers replaced Larry Riley as Golden State's general manager, which means he chooses the players for the team. Myers was a reserve player at UCLA but wasn't good enough to make the NBA. Instead he went to law school and became a sports agent. The Warriors thought he was so good at negotiating contracts that they hired him to do it for them. Upon taking the job, he began drafting and signing players who were quick and athletic but also capable of playing more than one position. In fact, Bob Myers didn't believe much in the traditional, rigid layout of a starting lineup—point guard, shooting guard, small forward, power forward, center.

While not every player could play every position, he wanted guys who could play two or three. It's why he believed so much in Steph, who could bring the ball up and run the offense but also hit shots and even rebound better than you'd expect for a six-foot-three player. Often in the NBA, when a player doesn't have an obvious position to play, teams get scared away. Myers was different. He wanted those guys, the positionless players. Klay Thompson, Harrison Barnes, Draymond Green, Andre Iguodala, and newcomer Shawn Livingston, a versatile guard, all fit that description. He didn't care where they played, he just cared that they could play well.

Steve Kerr believed in the same philosophy, which is why his hiring as coach was so important for Golden State. He wanted the Warriors offense to be wide open, with all five players capable of running, dribbling, passing, and shooting. He felt that if the Warriors could spread defenses out and confuse their opponents, his players could get open shots.

More than anyone else, he wanted those shots to go to the team's best shooter, Steph.

The 2014–15 Warriors won their season opener over Sacramento by eighteen points. Then they beat the Lakers by twenty-three, a game in which Steph had thirty-one points and Klay scored forty-one. They beat Portland next and then took on the Clippers, their nemesis in the Pacific Division, and smoked them by seventeen, with Steph leading the way with twenty-eight points.

Just like that, the Warriors were on a tear. Coach Kerr believed in the players. The players believed in Coach Kerr. Draymond and Harrison became starters, but the team played together no matter who was on the court. Everyone shot. Everyone rebounded. Everyone defended. From mid-November through mid-December they reeled off sixteen consecutive victories and were 21–2 for the season.

In the Bay Area, Warriors tickets became nearly impossible to get. Those days of a half-empty Oracle Arena were gone. Every game was must-watch television, both in California and around the country, where fans on the East Coast were bleary-eyed at work or school the next day after staying up late to see what Steph and the guys would do.

Golden State wasn't just a winning team, they were a phenomenon. No one had ever seen an NBA team that fired in so many three-pointers or encouraged players to pull up on a breakaway to shoot a jumper. There were times Coach Kerr left his centers on the bench and used a lineup with no one taller than six-foot-eight.

"I think how fast we play, we shoot a lot of threes as well, so I'm sure that that's fun to watch," Steph said. "And definitely it's kind of an ode to our fan base, when you watch a game on TV and you see Oracle Arena and our fans and how loud and passionate they are for the game. It shows on TV, but it's even more crazy in person."

Steph was the man in the middle of it all, seemingly raising his game each night. He had thirty-four against Oklahoma City, forty against Miami, fifty-one against Dallas. He was no longer just another player or someone hoping to be noticed—he was among the biggest stars in the league. That year he received more votes for the all-star game than anyone, even beating out Kobe Bryant and LeBron James. "I never expected that," Steph said. Then, on all-star weekend he won the three-point contest for the first time in four tries.

After the all-star break, the Warriors kept winning. In March and April there was a twelve-game win streak. Every night it was something else, something bigger. By the end of the regular season, Steph had hit 286 three-pointers, breaking his own all-time record from the season before. Klay meanwhile made 239 threes, the Splash Brothers dominating the season. Steph averaged 23.8 points a game and Klay added 21.7. The Warriors went 67–15, one of the best records of all time.

None of it, Steph kept saying, meant a thing, though, if they didn't win the NBA championship. In fact, after a season like that, not winning the title would be an embarrassment. That was the pressure the Warriors faced entering the playoffs. They were expected to win a championship. But could they?

They swept the New Orleans Pelicans in the first round, with Steph averaging 33.8 points in the series. Memphis was a tougher opponent in round two, with the Grizzlies shocking the Warriors and taking an early 2–1 game lead. Then Golden State buckled down and won by seventeen, twenty, and thirteen in the following three games, with Steph going for over thirty twice in that stretch. Houston and star guard James Harden awaited in the Western

Conference finals, but the Rockets were no match. Golden State jumped to a 3–0 lead with Steph scoring thirty-four, thirty-three, and forty. It went on to win in five games.

Maybe the most memorable thing to happen in that series came after Game 1, when Steph went to the podium to speak to the media. Reporters wanted to ask him about the game and how he thought the series might go. Instead he brought along his daughter, Riley, who would turn three later that summer. She sat on his lap, laughed, smiled, and even spoke into the microphone. At one point, she told Steph he was being too loud while trying to answer a question. Fans watching at home, and later on YouTube, were charmed by Steph's cute daughter. Riley was an overnight sensation.

"She's a bigger star than I am now," Steph said, only half joking. "When we go out now they're all asking where she's at. We went to Toys 'R' Us the other day and little girls were asking their dad if they could talk to Riley because they saw her on TV."

To Steph, having Riley along was just a natural thing to do. He was always about family, and his family was an NBA family. He was the son of an NBA player. He was the brother of an NBA player, Seth, who made the league after starring in college at Liberty University and later as a transfer at Duke University. Why not get as much time with your children as possible?

Both off and on the court, Steph was excelling. Just before the NBA Finals were set to begin, Steph received the highest honor the league has to offer an individual player. He was named the league's Most Valuable Player. There was little question he deserved the award. Steph received one hundred first-place votes, beating out Harden, who got twenty-five, and LeBron, who had five.

For a kid who had always been told he wasn't good enough or big enough, a guy who just a couple of years prior wasn't sure his ankle would hold up or if he was really talented enough to be an impact star, this was the ultimate sign of acceptance. Steph didn't just belong—he was now deemed the best. When Steph went to the award ceremony, he wanted to make sure he thanked his family, his coaches, and his teammates. He knew he would never have succeeded without them. He also wanted to use the chance to share his faith and his story and offer advice for everyone listening, whether they played basketball or not.

"First and foremost, I have to thank my Lord and Savior, Jesus Christ, for blessing me with the talents to play this game, with the family to support me day in and day out," Steph said when accepting the award. "I'm His humble servant right now, and I can't say enough how important my faith is to how I play the game and who I am."

Then he got to his basketball journey.

"I was always the smallest kid on my team," Steph said. "I had a terrible, ugly catapult shot from the time I was fourteen because I wasn't strong enough to shoot over my head. I had to reconstruct that over the summer, and it was the worst three months of my life. I wasn't highly touted as a high school prospect. I had nobody really running, knocking on my door saying, 'Please, please, please come play for our school' until Coach McKillop called."

Then he wanted to motivate people, make them realize that greatness is within them if they are willing to fight for it.

"If you take time to realize what your dream is and what you really want in life, no matter what it is, whether it's sports or in other fields, you have to realize that there is always work to do. You want to be the hardest-working person in whatever you do, and put yourself in a position to be successful. Be the best version of yourself in anything that you do. You don't have to live anybody else's story. It doesn't matter where you come from, what you have or don't have, or what you lack."

As great of a day as it was to be named MVP, Steph kept reminding everyone that you don't play the game for the individual honors, the money, or the fame. You play to win, and Golden State had its greatest challenge ahead of them: Steph's old friend and now rival LeBron James and the Cleveland Cavaliers. It wasn't so long ago that LeBron had been the big star, dropping in to watch a young Steph, the "Baby-Faced Assassin" as he came to be known since he looked young for his age, play for Davidson in the NCAA tournament.

Now they were equals. Just a couple of MVPs. The Finals is no time for friendships, and Steph understood that. LeBron isn't just one of the best players in NBA history, he is one of the most ferocious competitors. He had won two NBA titles in Miami but never one during his time with his hometown Cavaliers. No sports team in Cleveland had won a title of any kind since the 1964 NFL Browns. The city was desperate for a champion, and LeBron was determined to be the player to deliver it.

The first game showed that this was a whole other level of challenge for Steph and the Warriors. Despite losing forward Kevin Love to a shoulder injury and having star guard Kyrie Irving fracture his kneecap during the game, the Cavs forced overtime at Oracle. Golden State prevailed in the end, but LeBron finished with forty-four points. Steph finished with twenty-six, but he hit just two three-pointers.

With Irving and Love gone for the series and Golden State up 1–0, a lot of media and fans began to say the Warriors would cruise to the title. Cleveland was now mostly just LeBron James.

But the thing about LeBron is that when he decides to turn it on, he's a one-man wrecking crew.

The Cavs shocked Golden State by winning Game 2 in Oakland and then Game 3 back in Cleveland to take a 2–1 series lead. Worse for Golden State, Steph wasn't playing very well. He shot just two of fifteen from behind the arc in Game 2 and was equally off-target for most of Game 3. The Finals is when stars have to shine, and LeBron was doing his part. He scored thirty-nine points, grabbed sixteen rebounds, and dished out eleven assists in Game 2. In Game 3, his stat line was forty, twelve, and eight. He was dominating. Steph was disappointing. All of a sudden, even with that MVP trophy in his possession, back came the doubters.

"You are kind of trying to figure it out: 'Why am I missing shots? Why are things going the way they're going?'" Steph said.

While technically Golden State wouldn't be eliminated if they lost Game 4 in Cleveland, it felt like a must-win for the Warriors. They didn't want to fall behind 3–1 and give LeBron three chances to win one game and steal the title. Like they had all season, Golden State relaxed and responded. Steph had twenty-two points and seven assists, and his shooting slump seemed over as the Warriors won easily, 103–82.

Back in Oakland for Game 5, it was more of the same. Steph scored thirty-seven points, including going seven of thirteen from three-point range. Maybe most impressively, he scored seventeen in the fourth quarter to put Cleveland away, 104–91. Then came Game 6 back in Cleveland, with Steph scoring twenty-five despite a tough night from three-point range. His clutch free throws in the final minutes ended the game, clinched the series, and sealed the title.

Golden State, after all those years, and Steph Curry, after all those questions, were champions.

0.6
CURRY
30
30

11
Record

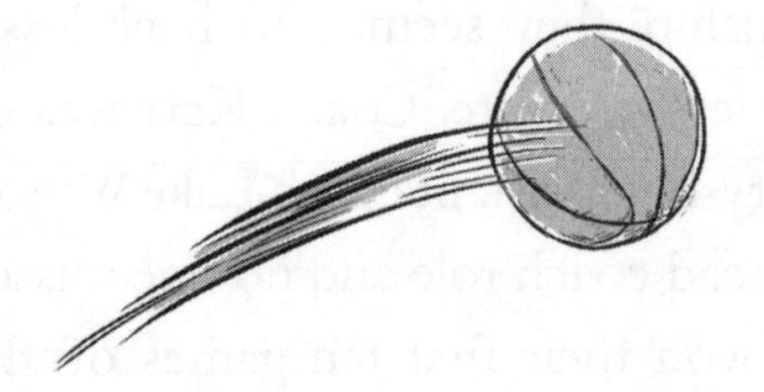

IF ANYONE THOUGHT the Golden State Warriors were going to lose their competitive drive the season after winning the championship, they couldn't have been more wrong.

On opening night of the 2015–16 season, Golden State raised their championship banner and received their championship rings. Once the celebration was over, it was right back to business.

That night they beat New Orleans by sixteen. Steph poured in forty. Two games later, he scored fifty-three as they kept racking up wins. The next game, "just" thirty, but the team beat Memphis by fifty. Golden State had been the greatest show in sports the previous year. Now they were headed to another level. They were 4–0 and their margin of victory was a combined one hundred points. The players were relaxed. Having already won a championship, they seemed to have less to prove and thus less pressure. Coach Kerr was out with a back injury, but assistant coach Luke Walton stepped into the head coach role and no one missed a beat.

They won their first ten games of the season. And then they won ten more after that! They started the year 24–0, an NBA record. Steph couldn't be stopped. He banged in forty-six against Minnesota and forty against the Clippers and forty-four against Toronto and so on and so on. He had become the most exciting and popular player in the league. Each night the Warriors played, stadiums sold out, viewership of games soared, and social media lit up with whatever highlight he produced. It was one thing for the Warriors to play before wild fans in Oakland, but now they were walking into enemy arenas and finding the stands filled up with Golden State jerseys, most often Steph's number 30.

Even before games began, fans arrived to witness Steph put on a spectacle—although he didn't see it that way. Videos had been appearing on YouTube of Steph's pregame warm-up routine. Some lucky fan or stadium worker who got in before the gates officially opened would film him going through a series of trick dribbles and long-range shots. Steph didn't do it for show; this was how he practiced and prepared. A lot of players do the same. His skill level was so high, though, and his shots fell from so far away, that it became mesmerizing. The Warriors, realizing that fans were now clamoring not just to see Steph play but to see Steph practice, began opening the arena up earlier so they could be there for his twenty-minute warm-up act.

Particularly popular was when Steph conducted a "two-ball drill" by dribbling a ball in each hand, alternating each one behind his back or through his legs like a street juggler. It was designed to get the feel for the ball and work on his ability to dribble equally well with both hands. Now it was filmed by a throng of fans pointing their phones at him. A routine he'd choreographed in the quiet of an empty practice facility now ended with cheers. When Steph was at home, he ended his warm-up by walking off the floor and into the tunnel only to have a security guard hand him a ball. He then heaved one up from the tunnel. More often than not, it went in even though he wasn't *even on the floor*.

With that much pregame excitement in Oakland, it wasn't long before opponents opened their arenas early, too, so their fans (or Golden State fans in their city) could take in the show as well. It got so popular that some local media tracked Steph's stats in *warm-ups*—"he hit 73 of 115 two-pointers," they reported.

"It's the same warm-up I've always done. I never thought it would become a big deal," Steph said. "It's not a show; it's how I prepare. Get the feel for the ball, work on shots I'll take in the game, loosen up my muscles. It's fun though."

It seemed everyone wanted to be like Steph, dress like Steph, and play like Steph. He was everywhere. There were commercials for Under Armour, of course. But also Degree deodorant, Brita water filters, Fanatics sports retail sales, and so on. You couldn't ignore him. One day he was playing ping-pong with Serena Williams for a Chase Bank commercial, the next day he was playing golf with President Barack Obama. Meanwhile, he was getting name-dropped nonstop in hip-hop tracks—by Drake, Nicki Minaj, Soulja Boy, Future, Fat Joe, Lil Wayne, Kehlani, and more.

He wasn't even the only celebrity in his house. Ayesha had always had a passion for cooking, and she used her talents to become a food blogger, a YouTube sensation, a cookbook author, and the host of her own show, *Ayesha's Homemade*, on the Food Network. Then, of course, there was Riley, who caused a stir wherever she went, and the newest addition to the Curry home, daughter Ryan.

Life may have sounded exciting, and it was, but for the Currys, some of their favorite times were just quiet ones at home, cooking a dinner and then watching a family movie with the kids. Steph and Ayesha wanted to maintain whatever level of normalcy they could. They may have become rich and famous, but they still saw themselves as two kids from Charlotte who met at a middle school Bible study.

On the court, Steph was redefining the way the game was played. Sure, his three-point shooting stats were incredible in terms of volume and accuracy, among the best ever, but there have been tons of great three-point shooters in NBA history. What set Steph apart was that the distance he was shooting from was often way beyond the arc. The three-point line is, at most, twenty-three feet, nine inches from the basket. In 2015–16 he shot forty-five from what statisticians measured to be at least thirty feet from the basket. That meant Steph was standing about seven feet behind the line and shooting anyway. Normally, this is a low-percentage shot, which is why it is rare that anyone takes more than a few a season. Not for Steph; he made twenty-one of his thirty-foot-plus shots that season—a ridiculous 46.7 percent.

When Golden State finally lost following their twenty-four-game run, they shrugged it off and won five more in a row. After they lost the next time, they went on to win seven consecutive games.

The victories piled up, but they weren't always easy. In late February, carrying a 52–5 record, the Warriors visited Oklahoma City. The Thunder were intent on beating Golden State and showing that the Western Conference title would be a true fight. The game went to overtime and was tied at 118 apiece when Steph got the ball in the backcourt with about five seconds remaining. He began pushing the ball up court with Oklahoma City's Andre Roberson, a lanky, six-foot-seven guard, trying to stay in front of him.

Everyone expected Steph to either drive to the hoop, pull up at the three-point line and shoot, or pass it to a teammate. Instead Steph took one dribble past half-court and surprised Roberson and everyone else by pulling up for a thirty-seven-foot three-pointer—over *thirteen* feet behind the line. To almost any other player in the world this would be a terrible shot. For Steph? It dropped through the basket with just 0.6 seconds remaining to give Golden State the incredible victory. It was Steph's forty-sixth point of the night and set an NBA record for the most three-pointers made in a single game—a record Steph would later break himself.

"Honestly, it's not like I'm calibrating in my head, all right, thirty-eight feet, thirty-seven, thirty-six," Steph said after. This was all about years of practice and just feeling confident to take a shot that may not look makeable but is for him. "I've shot the shot plenty of times before," Steph said.

No one could stop the Warriors, even though playing them became the game of the year for other teams. Soon fans and media were wondering if they could break the NBA's all-time record for wins in a season, seventy-two, held by the 1996 Chicago Bulls. Michael Jordan was the star of that team, but it also included Steve Kerr, who took great delight in having his new team chase his old team's record. He joked that if the two teams played a game, none of his current Warriors would have been able to guard him. To break the record, Golden State would have to lose fewer than ten games throughout the entire season. The team took it as a challenge, something to keep them motivated on a cold January night while playing on the road in the Midwest.

In mid-March, the Warriors lost by eight at San Antonio and were 62–7 on the season. They could only afford to lose two more games out of a total of twelve. The players promised to go all out to get the record. They responded by winning six consecutive games to get to 68–7. Then they lost to Boston at home, beat Portland by twenty-five, and then got shocked by Minnesota at home. They were now 69–9, with four games remaining and no margin for error. That included two games against San Antonio, one of the best teams in the league. And one of those was on the road in Texas. "Keep pushing the envelope," Steph told his teammates.

They beat San Antonio at home, survived a game

in Memphis by one, and then came back and beat San Antonio again. Each game was drawing huge national television audiences, America wondering if the Warriors could pull off the historic run.

The finale came at home against a good Memphis team, but Golden State wasn't going to be denied. They pounded the Grizzlies, leading by twenty-three at one point before settling in for a twenty-one-point victory before a crazed Oracle Arena. Steph had forty-six points, including ten of nineteen three-pointers, which was another milestone. He finished the season with 402 three-pointers, shattering his own three-point record (yet again) by 116. The number was unfathomable, a cartoonish figure that no one ever thought possible in the NBA. No other player had ever hit 300, and just three years prior the record had been 269. Now he was breaking the 400 barrier. Only a few players had even *attempted* 400 three-pointers in a season, let alone made them. It was video game–level stuff. For Steph, the record was proof that hard work paid off. "That's why I shoot all the reps that I do, and go out and play the way that I do," Steph said after the record was broken.

The wildest part? He was just one half of the

Splash Brothers. Klay drained 276 three-pointers himself, the most of any player in NBA history not named Stephen Curry. The Warriors had fully embraced Coach Kerr's style, and the rest of the NBA was still trying to adjust. No team had ever shot so many threes. Over the course of the 2015–16 season, playoffs included, Steph attempted 886 three-pointers, making 45.5 percent of them. In his first three seasons in the NBA combined, he'd attempted only 843 from behind the arc. This was the same talent but a new way of playing.

Steph was named MVP for the second consecutive season, becoming just the eleventh player to ever win the award back-to-back. He averaged 30.1 points a game and led the league in (of course) three-pointers made, free-throw percentage (.908), and steals (2.1), which illustrated his defensive mindset. As the best player on the best team in NBA regular-season history—there was no doubt in voters' minds—Steph was unanimously selected, receiving all 131 first-place votes. San Antonio's Kawhi Leonard finished second. LeBron came in third.

Steph said what he learned in winning a second MVP was the power of being around positive people who continue to encourage him rather than let him coast on what was already accomplished or try to tear him down due to jealousy. He believed that's a lesson for anyone whether it's in school, work, or sports.

"I tried to surround myself with people that push me, that motivate me, that keep me focused on the right things in this life," Steph said. "Everybody's given a certain skill set, a certain talent, a certain passion. To hold on to that and work as hard as you can to be the best that you can at what you feel like your place in this world is and what your role is. I learned at an early age that basketball is something I'd love to do every single day. But like every single person, just find what you're good at and work as hard as you can."

As the playoffs began, Golden State understood the pressure they were under. Winning seventy-three was incredible, but if they didn't win the championship, they would always feel a pang of regret. Tom Brady, the great quarterback of the New England Patriots, grew up in the Bay Area, in the city of San Mateo. He always kept an eye on the Warriors. Tom has won five Super Bowls. He told some on the Patriots, however, that he never got over one particular year when he didn't win it all. That was the 2007 season, when New England became the first NFL team to go 16–0 in the regular season, only to lose in the Super Bowl.

But it was smooth sailing for the Warriors early on in the playoffs. Golden State beat both Houston and then Portland in five games each to quickly move to the Western Conference finals. There waiting for them was the rival Oklahoma City Thunder, led by deadly scorers Kevin Durant and Russell Westbrook, two of the top players in the league.

Steph was battling a knee injury and had played in only four of the Warriors' first ten playoff games. He was a little rusty and not shooting well. Oklahoma City, which was not impressed by the Warriors' seventy-three wins or Steph's two MVP trophies, seized on that, jumping out to a 3–1 series lead, including easy victories in games three and four, where they defeated Golden State by twenty-eight and twenty-four respectively. Steph was a mess, hitting just five of twenty-one three-pointers in those two games. The NBA was shocked that Golden State, after their incredible regular-season performance, might not even make The Finals.

Not so fast.

The team rallied. Steph, no stranger to clutch

situations, stepped up, scoring thirty-one in Game 5, thirty-one in Game 6, and thirty-six in Game 7 to storm back from major trouble and win the series. Oklahoma City was crushed. Golden State went sailing into The Finals, where once again, LeBron and the Cleveland Cavaliers were waiting for them.

It was a rematch of the year before, but it was also different. This time Cleveland stars Kyrie Irving and Kevin Love were healthy. The challenge was greater, but Golden State appeared up for it.

They won three of the first four games, and Steph looked like he had overcome his knee injury from earlier in the playoffs. He hit seven of thirteen three-pointers in Game 4, scoring thirty-eight as the Warriors cruised. They needed just one more victory in three tries.

But there was another player on the court who knew how to step up in tight spots. A guy known as "King James."

LeBron went off for forty-one points, sixteen rebounds, and seven assists, and Kyrie scored forty-one more as the Cavs took Game 5. LeBron scored forty-one more as Cleveland won Game 6. That set up a Game 7 back in Oakland. It was one of the most anticipated games in NBA history. Even the players felt that way.

"I want . . . to enjoy the moment because growing up, playing with your friends, you kind of put yourself in so many Game 7s," Steph said. "This is my first crack at it."

Across the country, even the world, no one could get enough of Steph versus LeBron. The game was viewed on television by 30.8 million people in the United States alone, making it the most-watched NBA game in nearly a decade. The game was everything fans could have wanted, tight and intense throughout with two great teams battling back and forth. There were twenty lead changes and eleven ties, and neither team ever led by more than eight points. The fourth quarter was played at an incredible level. The defense was so tough that almost no one could make a shot. Steph struggled from outside and scored just seventeen. In the final minutes Kyrie Irving hit a critical three-pointer and LeBron had a huge blocked shot to allow Cleveland to pull away, 93–89. The dream season ended in a nightmare.

Steph was crushed. "It stung," he said. Yet as the Cavs celebrated on the Warriors' court, rather than retreat to the locker room in anger or disappointment, he and Andre Iguodala stuck around to watch as a sign of respect. When the Cavs were done jumping around, Steph and Andre made sure to shake all their hands. It was painful, but it was the right thing to do.

"It was tough to watch them celebrate, as we wished it would have been us," Steph said. "But at the end of the day, you congratulate them for accomplishing what they set out to do. That's all you can do . . . The competition was amazing in the series and that's what basketball is all about."

Steph had his moments in the playoffs and wouldn't make any excuses after, but his knee injury had slowed him. He wasn't the same player he'd been in that freewheeling regular season. His injured knee needed rest, which meant he had to drop out of the 2016 Olympic team, which he had been excited about. He wanted to win an Olympic gold medal. His near-perfect season had fallen apart.

12

Dynasty

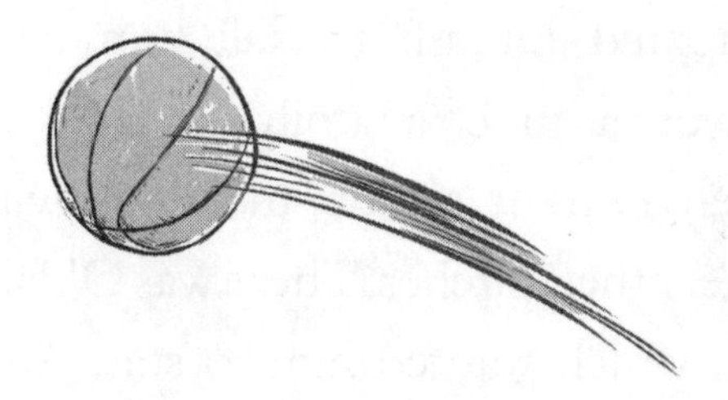

IT'S NOT EASY TO IMPROVE a team that won more regular-season games than any team in NBA history and came within a shot or two of winning the championship in Game 7 of The Finals. Golden State had talent, it had teamwork, it had chemistry, and it had coaching. What else could it possibly add?

An old rival, it turns out.

In July 2016, Kevin Durant, the six-foot-nine star of the Oklahoma City Thunder, was a free agent. He could choose to play for any team in the

NBA that had room under the salary cap to pay him. Golden State, it turned out, was one of those teams.

Durant loved the Bay Area, he loved Coach Kerr, and he loved the Warriors' unselfish style of play. He also loved the idea of teaming up with Steph Curry, another top-five player in the league, and chasing a championship. And Steph liked the idea, too. He texted Durant to sell him on how the Warriors were as much a family as a team. The proof came when Durant set up meetings with various teams to hear their pitches. There was Oklahoma City, of course, which wanted him to stay. And Boston, which wanted him on the East Coast. And there was Golden State, which sent to the meeting not just owner Joe Lacob, GM Bob Myers, and Coach Steve Kerr, but a bunch of the core players—Draymond, Klay, Iguodala, and Steph.

The all-out courtship worked. On July 4, 2016, Durant agreed to sign with the Warriors. Around the NBA, fans and media began complaining that Golden State was building an unfair super team, with players banding together to become unbeatable. Even league commissioner Adam Silver said he disliked the concept.

That wasn't fair, though. Yes, Golden State's

starting lineup would consist of four Western Conference all-stars from the season before—Steph, Klay, Draymond, and Kevin Durant. However, Steph, Klay, and Draymond had all come to the team via the draft, and none was picked in the top six the year they came out. The team was built on smarts. Only Kevin Durant arrived as a free agent.

Still, a narrative was set. Golden State, which had been seen mostly as a fun, exciting, lovable team around the league, was now a bit of a villain. Other fans were jealous. The Warriors embraced it, Steph even enjoying having the league root against their potential success.

Expectations for the Warriors were through the roof. Steph tried to minimize them a little bit. They weren't going to go 82–0, and as much as this was a high-pressure situation, they'd been in this position before. "Our expectations are really, really high, which they should be," Steph said. "[But] there's no more pressure than there was last year."

The biggest challenge was incorporating a new outside shooter into the flow of the offense without having it hurt Steph's and Klay's games. The Warriors lost their opener against San Antonio, but there was no reason to panic. They went on to win sixteen of their next seventeen as everyone figured out how to make it work.

There were other changes afoot that season for Steph, including one that took place off the court. He turned twenty-nine and became comfortable using his voice and status as a two-time MVP to speak out on issues outside of just basketball. He was no longer some up-and-coming player. He was a global icon, with tens of millions of followers on Instagram, Twitter, and Snapchat. He supported San Francisco 49ers quarterback Colin Kaepernick's protest of racial inequality in America, even though Curry did not kneel during the national anthem at any NBA pregames. He also criticized Donald Trump for what Steph saw as the president's embrace of racial intolerance. He worked to challenge "what we tolerate in this country, what is accepted, and what we turn a blind eye to." He also increased his many charitable endeavors, raising money for hurricane victims, a family crisis center in North Carolina, and the Animal Rescue Foundation. He also worked with the United Nations on a project called Nothing But Nets, which helps provide protective nets for people in Africa dealing with the threat of malaria.

Not everything was charity. Ever since signing his second contract, Steph had been the best bargain in the NBA. He made $12.1 million that year, which was a lot, but LeBron James was paid $31 million. Steph didn't complain, but he was happy when at the end of the season Golden State signed him to a new, five-year deal worth $201 million, an average of $40.2 million per year. At the time, it was the richest contract in NBA history.

Golden State went 67–15 for the season, and while they didn't challenge the all-time single-season victory mark, that was somewhat of a relief. The prior year, the Warriors had expended a lot of physical and mental energy chasing the record. Steph averaged 25.3 points a game. Kevin Durant followed with 25.1. Klay added 22.3. Steph scored about five fewer points a game than in 2015–16 and hit seventy-eight fewer three-pointers, but it hardly mattered. His 324 threes was still the second-most ever. He was happy to share the ball with Kevin Durant a little if it meant achieving the ultimate goal.

"We're here to win a championship," Steph said. "That's it. That's why we play, to realize that dream. We know, having won before, we know exactly what it takes. Having been on the losing side, we know how thin the line is between winning and losing . . . I don't want to feel what I felt last year and I'm going to do everything in my power to attack every game with that kind of perspective."

"Attack" is a good way of describing what happened next. In the first round of the playoffs, they swept Portland by an average margin of eighteen points a game. In the second round, they swept Utah by an average of fifteen points a game. In the Western Conference finals, they swept San Antonio by an average of sixteen points a game. This wasn't a playoff run as much as a tank rolling over a cardboard house. There were so many weapons, so many possibilities, that the Warriors couldn't be stopped. When Golden State needed Steph to score forty, he scored forty. When someone else had a hot hand, he sat back and played a supporting role. Even after all these years, all the accolades, people in the NBA still saw him improving his game.

"He has the wisdom to make his game be even more solid, a little bit less mustard, and a little bit more fundamentally sound, which reduces turnovers, gets more shots for teammates," San Antonio coach Gregg Popovich said. "So, he's been willing to tone it down a little bit over the past few years, and possessions are that much more powerful. Obviously, his confidence has gone through the roof because he realizes that what he does is special."

Waiting in The Finals, once again, were Cleveland and LeBron. This would be the third consecutive matchup between the two franchises, and it was fitting. Each had won one. Golden State still wanted revenge from the year before, when they'd lost despite leading 3–1 to start the series. And Steph and LeBron were ready for another match—two all-time great players even though they played different styles.

This time, it was no contest. Adding Durant to the Warriors altered the balance completely. Game 1, it was the Warriors by twenty-two as Steph scored twenty-eight and Kevin Durant thirty-eight. Game 2, it was the Warriors by nineteen as Steph had thirty-two and Durant thirty-three. Game 3 was in Cleveland, the last real chance for the Cavs to make it a competitive series. The Warriors won by five. Durant had thirty-one, Klay thirty, and Steph twenty-six.

Golden State became the first team in NBA history to win fifteen consecutive playoff games. They were one victory from a perfect 16–0 record, which would have been a first. Except Cleveland rose up and won Game 4 on pride, stopping Golden State's chance at history. Game 5 back in Oracle became a coronation, with Steph scoring thirty-four and Kevin Durant thirty-nine and the Warriors winning their second championship in three seasons.

They weren't done, either. For Golden State, the 2017–18 season was about proving they could repeat as champions. The Warriors knew they had the talent, but it takes a lot more than just talent to win a championship. Players have to stay healthy. They have to continue to listen to their coach and one another. They have to work as hard and remain as hungry as they were before they ever won a championship. And they have to hold off other teams that are trying to upset them: in this case, the Houston Rockets.

Houston featured star players James Harden, Chris Paul, and Eric Gordon. The Rockets had spent the previous couple of years building themselves up, and now they were focused on proving they could knock off Golden State and win an NBA title. The NBA scheduled Houston to play Golden State on the opening night of the season, and after the Warriors received their championship rings and hung another banner from the Oracle rafters, Houston showed that this was a new season. It upset Golden State, 122–121, setting the tone for the year. Houston would boast the best regular season record in the NBA, 65–17, including going 2–1 against the Warriors. There was a stretch in the middle of the season when Houston went 28–1. It looked formidable. Golden State, meanwhile, struggled at times, winning "just" fifty-four games and going 7–10 to end the season.

Part of the problem was Steph, who suffered repeated ankle sprains and had to sit out at times during the season. There was concern that his old injuries were back and he might not get healthy for the playoffs. Although he averaged 26.4 points a game, tied with Durant for tops on the team, he appeared in just fifty-one of eighty-two regular season games and sat out the Warriors' first six games of the playoffs. By the time Houston and Golden State matched up in the Western Conference Finals, Steph was still trying to get back to form. In the first two games, which the teams split, he shot just two of thirteen from three-point range and averaged just seventeen points a game. That wasn't good enough. Not if the Warriors wanted to repeat as champions.

Then came Game 3 and Steph delivered a thirty-five-point barrage in a Golden State blowout. Just like that, the rust was off and the rehab was done. The old Steph returned. He was flying to the hoop. He was nailing step-back threes. He was frustrating opponents who couldn't figure out how to stop him. Even as Houston took a 3–2 series lead and had two chances to knock the Warriors off, Steph and his teammates remained confident.

And for good reason. Steph had twenty-nine in a Game 6 come-from-behind victory. In Game 7 in Houston, the Rockets took a 54–43 lead at halftime and were outplaying the Warriors. Steph was just 3 of 10 from the floor. The fans in Houston were loud and rowdy, sensing this might be it. Perhaps, finally, the Warriors' time had ended, and the Rockets' had come.

Rather than panic, though, Golden State rallied in the locker room and reminded one another to trust their talent and teamwork. "You've got to have resiliency," Steph said. "You've got to have confidence in yourself, no matter how the game's going, that you can turn it around."

Turn it around they did. Golden State went on a tear and Curry delivered a flurry of points, hitting five of six shots, including four of five from behind the arc in the third quarter alone as the Warriors took the lead. During one stretch, he scored eleven consecutive Golden State points. In the biggest moment of the season, he was at his best, finishing with twenty-seven for the game as Golden State cruised to victory, survived their latest challenge, and advanced to their fourth consecutive NBA Finals. "This is a true testament to how hard it is to get to The Finals," Steph said.

LeBron and the Cavaliers were waiting again in The Finals, but this Cleveland team was weaker than the previous ones. LeBron was still LeBron, but Kyrie Irving had been traded and the supporting cast wasn't strong. Game 1 went to overtime, but after Golden State survived and won, it never faltered again. Steph averaged 27.5 points a game in The Finals, including a dizzying thirty-seven-point performance in the closeout game to sweep Cleveland, 4–0. Just like with their first NBA title, the Warriors celebrated in Cleveland. "I'm just extremely grateful," Steph said.

For Steph, becoming a three-time NBA Champion was another sign of him entering his prime as an NBA superstar on a team capable of winning the championship for years to come. The days of overlooked high school player or uncertain young player on some weak Warriors teams were almost hard to recall. Except Steph would never forget. "I'll remember for a very long time," he said. "From the depths of the NBA to here to world champs again. It's crazy."

That's how he avoids complacency, embraces new challenges, and continues to grow. The path to greatness is never simple, even for Stephen Curry.

Instant Replay

118
05.3
118
FEBRUARY 27, 2016: Steph Curry gets the ball with seconds left in a tie game vs. Oklahoma City.

30
30
STEPH RECEIVES THE PASS AND DRIBBLES DOWN THE COURT.

STEPH MAKES HIS
WAY TO MIDCOURT
WITH JUST SECONDS
LEFT IN THE GAME.
30

EVERYONE THINKS HE IS GOING TO DRIBBLE CLOSER TO THE BASKET.

INSTEAD, STEPH SURPRISES THE DEFENSE BY SQUARING UP TO SHOOT.
CURRY
30

IT'S JUST LIKE HE'S A KID AGAIN, IN HIS DRIVEWAY TAKING PRACTICE SHOTS, DREAMING OF ONE DAY PLAYING IN THE NBA.

02.5
STEPH RELEASES THE SHOT FROM THIRTY-SEVEN FEET AWAY FROM THE BASKET!
02.4
CURRY
30

02.3

THE BALL SAILS THROUGH THE AIR TOWARD THE HOOP.

02.2

01.9
30
30
THE CROWD LOOKS ON AS THE CLOCK TICKS DOWN.
01.7
CURRY
30
1.5

STEPH SINKS THE GAME-WINNING SHOT!
01.2

0.6
CURRY
30
GAME OVER! GOLDEN STATE WINS.

30

STEPH CURRY CELEBRATES
ANOTHER CLUTCH
THREE-POINTER.

The Nonstop Sports Action Continues!

Here's an excerpt of

EPIC ATHLETES
KEVIN DURANT

Illustrations by Marcelo Baez

2017 NBA Finals Game 3
GS CLE
111 113
4th 52.3
DURANT
35

1
The Shot

IT WAS THE FINAL MINUTE of the fourth quarter of Game 3 of the 2017 National Basketball Association (NBA) Finals and a single basket—or rebound, steal, missed shot, or turnover—by either team could swing not just this neck-and-neck contest, but potentially the entire championship. The Cleveland Cavaliers led the Golden State Warriors, 113–111 in a matchup that was about as close and tense as basketball can get.

Golden State had jumped to a 2–0 lead in the best-of-seven Finals, but heading into this contest, the Warriors knew better than to get overconfident. Just a year prior they'd won seventy-three regular season games and led these same Cavs 3–1 in The Finals. They'd looked like one of the greatest teams in NBA history. Then LeBron James led a historic comeback that saw Cleveland win Games 5, 6, and 7 and take the NBA championship.

Now a year later, late in Game 3, every single Warriors player, coach, and fan had to wonder if LeBron might do enough to win this game and steal another championship from Golden State.

That's when Kevin Durant reached up high with his long, long right arm and snatched a missed Cleveland shot out of the air. Suddenly Golden State was on the offensive with a chance to tie—or take the lead.

Moments like this were exactly why the Warriors had brought Kevin to the team. And this was exactly the type of moment Kevin had hoped would come when he'd signed with Golden State. He hadn't played for the Warriors in 2015–16 when they'd fallen short of winning The Finals. In the offseason that followed, Golden State signed Kevin as a free agent because the team felt it lacked one more player who could come up big in the sport's loneliest of moments—when the pressure of roaring fans and high stakes cause nerves to fray. They felt they needed someone who could close out games, like tonight, and thus would ensure that another LeBron-style comeback never happened again.

Officially Kevin is listed at six foot nine, but he's admitted that in his signature Nikes, he stands seven feet tall. He said he likes being listed as shorter than his true height as a joke, part of his fun, free-spirited personality.

He'd always been the tallest anyway—the tallest in his class in kindergarten, fourth grade, and middle school. He was this skinny kid who kept growing and growing and growing while being raised in Prince George's County, Maryland, just outside of Washington, DC. As much as his height helped him become a talented basketball player, it was his arms that set him apart even in the NBA, where almost everyone is tall.

With his arms stretched out, Kevin's wingspan measured seven foot five end to end, and somehow he was still coordinated. He could shoot and dribble like someone a foot shorter. Yet he could rebound and block shots in a way no six-foot guard could even dream of doing.

So snagging that rebound was the easy part. What to do next was the tougher decision.

There were about fifty-one seconds remaining in the game. Golden State needed a basket. It needed a hero.

Kevin had always felt he was built for these kinds of make-or-break scenarios. His combination of size and skill made him nearly impossible to defend. He felt that when his team needed to score, he was the one capable of doing it, especially in big games.

Yet getting to the ultimate pressure-filled stage, The Finals, had proven difficult for him throughout his career. He'd spent eight years playing for the Oklahoma City Thunder (and one year prior when the team had been based in Seattle and was called the SuperSonics). He'd reached one NBA Finals in 2012, but lost to LeBron, who was playing for Miami then.

Kevin was twenty-two years old at the time and thought he'd return regularly to The Finals.

He didn't. Oklahoma City always fell short. Sometimes it was in the Western Conference Finals. Sometimes it was due to injury. Whatever it was, Kevin couldn't get the NBA championship that he coveted.

He noted that he'd spent his entire basketball life in second place. He'd been ranked the number two high school player in the country. He was the number two pick in the 2007 NBA draft. He finished, for years, at number two in the NBA's MVP voting (although he eventually won the award in 2014). He was always the runner-up, and never the champion. After ten years in the league, he'd made millions of dollars and acquired millions of fans, he'd starred in movies and television commercials, he was huge on social media, and he had become active in charitable giving.

The one thing he didn't have, however, was an NBA title.

He wanted one so desperately that he left Oklahoma City, where he was a beloved fan favorite and life was comfortable, to join the powerhouse Warriors in Oakland, where he needed to adjust his game and mentality to fit in with other established players. At Golden State, he wouldn't be the most popular player (that was Steph Curry), but he thrived on being part of a true team that could win it all.

So now he had not just the ball in his hand but destiny as well. Over twenty thousand Cavaliers fans were beginning to shout inside of the Quicken Loans

Arena in downtown Cleveland, screaming to distract Kevin as he took the ball and began dribbling it up the court. "De-fense!" they chanted. "De-fense!"

That Kevin was able to masterfully handle the ball, at such a height, was a wonder that had become commonplace. He made it look easy, but in the rich history of basketball, there may never have been a player this tall who could dribble so well. There may never have been a seven-footer who could so effortlessly take over the role of point guard in an instant.

It had begun back in Prince George's County, at a simple city recreational building in his hometown of Seat Pleasant. It was in Seat Pleasant that Kevin grew up with his older brother, Tony, raised mostly by his mother and grandmother (his father would reenter his life later). It was there that he met a couple of youth basketball coaches, Taras Brown and Charles Craig.

While they saw a kid who was taller than the other players, they didn't teach him the game in the traditional way. They didn't want Kevin to just play down low and grab rebounds, or learn only to score around the basket, as is the case for most power forwards and centers. He was too athletically gifted for that and his coaches saw that the sport of basketball was changing.

They taught Kevin how to play all the positions, including schooling him on dribbling, passing, and shooting from a distance by putting him through endless, repetitive drills. Dribbling through cones. Dribbling with both hands. Dribbling two balls at once. Dribbling, dribbling, dribbling.

Then they'd move on to shooting practice. Shot after shot, day after day, year after year. It was a basketball science project, like they were creating the perfect player in a lab. And Kevin was all for it, a tireless worker who understood that there were no shortcuts to becoming truly great.

Each repetition slowly caused his muscles to memorize the kind of form and touch that would never abandon him—even when his team needed a basket and he knew it wasn't just all those Cleveland fans watching him, but the entire basketball world.

As Kevin pulled that rebound out of the air and brought it down to his body, he spun his head and saw open space in front of him. The Cavaliers were charging back to play defense, to guard against the Warriors whipsaw offense that called for players to dart in all directions until someone got open. It might be Steph Curry, the two-time MVP. It might be Klay Thompson, the clutch three-point specialist. It might go down low to Draymond Green, who could power home a bucket.

No one knew at the moment that Kevin Durant, who had worked and waited his entire life for this chance, wasn't going to pass it to anyone. He thought back to his earliest days in the game, playing as a kid on a local Amateur Athletic Union (AAU) team, and knew what was expected of him.

"Every team I'm on, in order for us to go to the next level, I have to assert myself," Kevin said. "Since I was playing for the [Prince George's] Jaguars when I was ten years old, I felt like if I didn't assert myself, we weren't as good as we should be."

Which was just fine with his teammates.

"We know in that situation to get that man the rock," Klay Thompson said. "He's seven foot, can shoot over almost anybody, and has amazing shooting touch."

With a single focus in mind, Kevin started up the court, his long strides covering huge swaths of hardwood. One dribble. Two dribbles. No one from Cleveland rushed up to stop him. A third dribble and he was now past the half-court line.

LeBron was waiting at the three-point line, but was slowly retreating, giving Kevin more room. Clearly LeBron thought Kevin, with his team down two points, would drive to the hoop and try to tie the game. Kevin had other ideas.

"I [saw] him backing up and I just wanted to take that shot," Kevin said.

He took a fourth dribble and casually slowed his run, as if he were about to stop and set up the offense. It was enough for LeBron to relax, ever so slightly. Yet when Kevin approached the three-point line, he didn't stop and look to pass, he just set his size eighteen Nikes down twenty-six feet from the basket and pulled up to shoot.

LeBron, a beat too late, tried to react and leaped at Kevin with an outstretched arm that sought to at least harass Kevin into a miss. Kevin didn't even notice. His jumper was so smooth, so textbook, he just rose and fired.

"I just tried to stay disciplined in my shot, hold my follow-through," Kevin said.

The ball soared toward the hoop in a perfect arc.

Swish.

It was the shot of a lifetime after a lifetime of making shots.

"Durant from three!" said the announcer on ESPN. "It's good. Kevin Durant from downtown as Golden State takes the lead."

Warriors 114. Cavaliers 113.

"KD said, 'I've been working on that shot my entire life,'" Steph Curry said after. "Literally that's his mindset—'I'm ready to take this shot because I haven't cheated the game. I put the time in every year to get better . . . and to be ready for those kind of moments.'"

Seconds later Cleveland's Kyrie Irving would miss a shot. Then Kevin would get fouled and sent to the line, where he made both free throws to extend the Warriors' lead. Cleveland missed again and then Steph salted away the game when he hit two more free throws.

Golden State celebrated a 118–113 victory and a commanding 3–0 lead in the NBA Finals.

Two games later, they closed the series out and Kevin Durant became a champion, at last. He was named NBA Finals MVP. He was no longer second best at anything.

"It feels," Kevin said after, "so great."

Hungry for More EPIC ATHLETES?
Look Out for These Superstar
Biographies, in Stores Now!